SEEN THROUGH OUR EYES

SEEN
THROUGH
OUR
EYES

edited by
Michael
Gecan

introduction by
Charles A. Reich

RANDOM HOUSE
NEW YORK

To
our
parents

INTRODUCTION

Almost everything that has been written about the new generation is by older people—professors, psychiatrists, intellectuals, an occasional leader of a radical organization who is himself out of college. These commentators bring their own terms to their writing, a frame of reference from their own experience that simply does not fit the new experience of youth. So the new generation has been written about but seldom understood.

The purpose of this book is to allow the reader to listen to some authentic voices of the new generation, talking about their own lives, how they experience things, how they see America, what they feel. Writing is not the most effective language of youth, and any book such as this is a compromise, an introduction, at best a beginning. It is an attempt to begin communication.

Several books and articles by young people have appeared during the last year or two, but almost all of those writings deal with the more journalistically appealing aspects of the so-called counterculture. Thus we have reports on hitchhiking, drugs, demonstrations, and political movements. The present essays are on a very different level. They show aspects of ordinary life. The changes in ordinary life are not as sensational, but they are much deeper and much more important. All too often the counterculture is merely a "trip." The writers here are telling about a transformation in day-to-day living that is more permanent. Sometimes the activity is the same as before, but the feeling or understanding is different. Such changes escape the superficial eye of the media. But it is just these changes that really matter, that really are transforming our society.

Understanding the new generation is in part a problem of understanding new languages. The terms in which older writers except to interpret any social movement are political and ideological. They look for a critique, a rational argument, a structure, a system. But the new generation is concerned with something altogether different, a way of seeing, of feeling, of experiencing the world, of communication, of knowing oneself.

Every human activity—riding a bike, music, dance, swimming in the sea—is a language. Each expresses one side of human nature. Each is a source of energy, vitality, creativity. Each offers a way to communicate with other people. Each offers knowledge of self. None of these languages is interchangeable with any other. What can be said in music cannot be said by cooking eggs and bacon, and neither can be said by words. And each language enriches and multiplies the other.

In our present society, these languages are shunted aside, and men are forced to attempt to express themselves and communicate through jobs and roles and technological skills. But all of these are alienated from man, so they are not real languages. And conversation, if it is based on alienated experience, is equally sterile. There is then no way to communicate, no way to have experiences together or to know oneself.

When the new generation creates its own music, or studies yoga, or seeks out nature as a source, it is rediscovering old languges and creating new ones, and thus repossessing the sources of human vitality that have been suppressed so long. People who have hardly met each other can nevertheless feel some of the deep sharing of long-time friendship, because they share experiences and language. They are like old friends who have been through many experiences together, but with the new languages those experiences can be shared by many people.

To accept and listen to new languages is not easy for anyone. The first time I saw men with shoulder-length hair the idea was too much for me. The first time I heard electrified guitars at full amplification it seemed like some hellish Walpurg is Night. It is not easy to hear the message even when the words are in English; I bought Bob Dylan's records as they came out, but it took years for me really to listen. All along the way to these new languages, I had a lot of help. But even with all that help, I cannot hear rock or blues as easily and naturally as those who have grown up in it.

For anyone who wants to learn the new languages, something more than intellectual effort is needed. One must have the help of individuals—friends who do not merely talk about their ideas, but embody them, at least to a degree. So the essential thing in reading this book is to try to know the individual writers, at least insofar as one can know them through writing.

The first part of the book suggests how some young people experience and respond to the everyday facts of contemporary America. Their primary experience is not with dramatic things like the war, but with such ordinary matters as growing up in a clean, modern, suburban house with one of those lawns we see on television, attending school and succeeding in it, getting a job and encountering realities on the job, playing basketball before a hostile crowd. The first personal response to contemporary Amer-

ica is likely to be anger, discouragement, or apathy. And
so this part of the book ends with Scott Stoner's lonely
nighttime walk around New Haven streets and Bill Littlefield's friend who just can't face the world at all.

The middle section of the book shows how something
positive begins. There are no political or economic pro-
posals here, and no one goes out to work in an election
campaign or rings doorbells to get people to recycle waste.
The positive may be the joy of a motorcycle, or the growth
of a new personal dimension, or a profoundly educational
experience with drugs. These experiences are all rather
obvious, well known, and highly publicized. But side by
side with them we find a transformation that is so subtle
that it may escape notice altogether. This is the growth
of awareness and the expansion of the ability to love. Read
Jonathan Sternberg's sensitive, humorous, compassionate
report on the conflicts and pathos at a summer swimming
pool for the middle-class aged. And Leigh Crystal's experience of meeting a possible boyfriend and eventually learning about the world of the homosexual. In each case, what
is most important is what is happening to the writer's own
head: we are able to watch these two individuals growing
through the experiences which they describe. Youth in
America has traditionally been an age of intolerance, of
differences, of forced conformity. Yet here we see the development of an ability to understand and to cherish
things that many adults can neither appreciate nor accept.
That opening up of the self is the real inner revolution.

The last part of the book takes us beyond particular
experiences to the search for new patterns of life. Here
again great changes are expressed not like politicians'
speeches but in highly personal terms. To Peter Mareneck
the search means creating a new family, one where life

is "subjectivized," that is, the numbers share their inner
selves with each other. To Michael Gecan it means rediscovering his own family, his father and mother and their
Croatian heritage. To Charles Levin it is the larger human
family: "You are my teacher. I am yours."

I should say a few words about the origin and arrangement of the book. All of these essays were written by
Yale undergraduates for a course I formerly taught en-
titled "The Individual in America" and known as American
Studies 36a. No topics were assigned; these are simply
some of the most interesting papers, chosen out of a much
greater number and arranged in the order they seem to
require. The editor, Michael Gecan, was first a student in
the class and later assisted in reading the papers.

Behind these undergraduate papers lies a transformation in life and society so profound as to be a revolution for which we have no words. I can remember the
1950s in Washington, D.C.—cynical, lonely, forlorn
times. We did not believe in anything, not in Eisenhower's
America, not in our work, or each other, or ourselves. The
world was like a stifling hot Washington day, no sky, no
horizon, no breeze, no energy or vitality anywhere, as
sterile as the bureaucratic marble of Washington's official
buildings. We could talk, we could eat lunch in a group,
we could gather for drinks in someone's backyard, but we
could not share anything, we could not be together, we
could not even feel alive. That gleaming city was Bob Dylan's *Desolation Row,* Norman Mailer's *Deer Park,* Fellini's
Dolce Vita, Eliot's *Waste Land,* a place where one felt oneself dying. Who can put into words the miracle of life
being reborn into such a sterile world, of idealism, courage, humor, hope, love? The rebirth of a future which
none of us believed in?

These papers cannot put such a miracle into words. All they attempt to do is to start a conversation. But communication is what this "revolution" is all about. Many people are saying that the youth movement in America has lost its momentum, that its culture is being co-opted, that the Establishment is stronger than ever. This comes from expecting the wrong revolution, from not speaking the new languages. If we recognize that the beginning of change is growth of awareness, of knowledge, of ways of communicating, then we can recognize that the process of change is growing ever stronger.

The first stage of change was spectacular: the new freedom, the rejection of the old, the new means of communication, especially rock, the pain and ecstasy of new space. But deeper change is quieter. Many of the students who participated in Yale's 1970 May Day politicization felt discouraged afterward, like Bill Boly. But the object was to insure that Bobby Seale and other black revolutionaries got a fair trial and that objective was fulfilled a year later; who can say that the demonstrations did not help make the trials more scrupulously fair? Bill Littlefield's hero, David, just wants to sleep, but that is quite natural when all the opportunities for doing something seem, in our over-organized society, to require the doing of evil; I think David will wake up when he finds work he can do that will be good for himself and for society. Just the other day I was out at Peter Mareneck's commune on Skokorat Road, looking at the first green shoots of their vegetable garden coming up under the watchful eye of a marvelously funny scarecrow: the growing process did not make a sound and change was invisible to the eye, but it was happening.

I think that in a true sense Peter Mareneck and the

other authors of this book are rediscovering America. Our gigantic institutions, brutal wars, and our alienation from each other and ourselves have taken us far away. But now we are beginning to rediscover our native land, its soil, its culture, and its people, the real things that are still there outside the unreal structures and systems that have distorted our lives for so long. We are beginning to recall the vision of America, and it is not some lurid super-hype in psychedelic colors, but a bean plant grown at Skokorat commune by some kids from Yale who are learning—relearning—how to live with the earth and with each other.

The slow and arduous task of creating a new life is not one for youth alone. It is one that everyone must undertake: the times allow us no choice, no way to avoid this. It is not something that any of us should have to face alone. Yet there is great danger that the new generation will simply depart whether others come along or not: "We are leaving, you don't need us," they say. But that need not be. These essays are an invitation to share, to recognize that the new awareness includes everybody, is possible for everybody; or that, in Charles Levin's words

You are always
welcome in my house.

Come in. Listen.

Charles A. Reich
New Haven, June 1, 1971

CONTENTS

Charles A. Reich   Introduction   vii

PART I

David Darlington   Work   3
Daniel Peters   Why We *Are* In Vietnam   11
John S. Rolander   This is the "Real World"?   31
Donald D. Lindley   My Friend Chuck   47
Mary Wilke   All I Wanted Was To Sing   59
Scott Stoner   In Search of Cockaigne   69
Bill Littlefield, Jr.   David: A Fantasy in One Act   87

PART II

Robert Walker   Life is What You Make It   101
Leigh Crystal   An Encounter   109
Charles A. Pidano, Jr.   Metamorphosis   123
Robert H. Rettew   Another Night   135
Thomas E. Seus   T.S. at Yale   149
Jonathan Sternberg   The Summer at Franklin Arms   161
Ralph Halsey   Alexander   175

PART III

Peter Mareneck   A Letter to Home   185
Charles H. Levin   Hello . . .   197
William Boly   How I Won my Major Why   205
Michael Gecan   Family Journeys: Sights Seen   219

About the Contributors   239

PART

WORK

by
David
Darlington

It's sunny out, damn it. I can tell by the streak of sunlight down by my legs. Well, if it were raining we'd just have to put it off and we might as well get it over with. Maybe it's windy, though; if it is, we can't burn . . . nope. Not one leaf or branch is moving. Shit. Shit, I'll say it again, shit, shit, shit, shit. Doesn't he understand? I go to school five days in a row and I do homework five nights in a row. The weekend is supposed to be for relaxation. Maybe he likes working out in this damn yard, but I happen to like playing football. I happen to *love* playing football, and it is a beautiful day. God, I hate the fall, I hate it! I hate those trees. A backyard full of trees. They're nice for shade in the summer, and they're pretty-looking, but that's about it. With that fence back there, the yard would be fantastic for baseball. We could have home plate in the corner by the garage, and it would be a natural field complete with home-run fence. How tremendous to put one over that fence . . . but the yard is all full of these damn trees that you can't even climb because they just go straight up with no branches for about thirty feet. I asked him for a basketball backboard, on one of the trees, back in the far corner where nobody'd see it. (He won't put one over the driveway because it would look ugly from the street.) But no, not in the back either, the grass would get wrecked. And I asked him for a tree house when I was little, so that maybe we could use the trees for *something* good. He said he'd do it Sunday. That was two hundred and fifty Sundays ago. It's not because he's lazy. God no, he's the un-laziest person in the world. He spends his whole life working. If it's not in New York during the week it's in the yard during the weekend. But why me? I'm not him. I don't like to work. Why does he force it on *me*? Well, there's no one else to help him, I guess; and he is getting a little old. Actually, he kills himself out there, and actually, I do very little compared to him. But that's because he's such a fanatic about it! Everything has to be perfect. As much time as I've put in out there, I know pretty little. I don't get taught anything; he does the tricky stuff himself, because the important thing, see, is that the lawn look nice.

God, I hate this time of year worse than anything. I can't look forward to football season because that means looking forward to leaf-raking season. I don't think it would be half as bad if it were just raking. But it is my job to clean out those planters and shrubbery. The dead leaves get caught in there and they just clog the whole thing up and choke it to death. And I have to clean it out by hand. The bushes are covered with sharp pine needles, and they prick your arms. But if you wear gloves, you can't pick the leaves up as easily. And there's *vermin* in there! When the leaves are wet you uncover these god-awful water bugs, the gray ones who have millions of scurvy little legs on the bottom. And last year, in the sand in the corner of the planter, there were anthills. Thousands of giant black ants running around. I had to stick my hands in there. He said, "They aren't gonna hurt ya." Shit. One day I'll uncover a boa constrictor, then we'll see.

It's always sunny out while I'm doing it, of course. Always beautiful. But my friends know by now that on Sundays they can forget about me. "I have to work." I have to admit, though, that it does give you a sort of perverse satisfaction. You sit there in the street picking at these leaves and a car goes by full of a father and the neighborhood kiddies, and they look like the flabbiest, softest, laziest bunch of goldbricks. They see you slaving and it's like having a sign with an arm and hammer on it up over the driveway: "WE WORK HERE." Yeah. My father tells me there's nothing like the feeling of having done an honest day's work. See, it's not just a question of getting up and getting out and getting it done; it's not like "keeping the place up." It's not carefree like that. It's an obsession—a moral issue between me and him. It's always been pretty obvious that he measures my mother's worth and mine by the amount of work we do. When she gets me up in the morning the first thing she tells me is how long he's already been outside and that I better hurry up and show him that I want to help. But I *don't* want to help! In the summer when it's grass-cutting instead of leaf-raking, it's like sinful for me to be in the house without going out there and making the token gesture of asking my father if I can relieve his mowing. But I don't *want* to relieve it! How did the most ambitious person in the world happen to give birth to the laziest person in the world? Or—was that an accident? Maybe that's the way it works. As a matter of fact, I'm sure of it. I know I wouldn't hate to work as much if it weren't for all this *moral demand*. He's always making it a big deal, he's always judging me on the basis of this lawnwork crap. "You better plan to be around here this weekend because you're gonna help me with these leaves." To him work isn't something you do just to do it, out of necessity; you do it because it is *honorable*. It's a damn religion!

What does he get from all of it? A nice-looking lawn. Most definitely. Ever since I can remember, an inherent factor around this family has been pride in the way the house looks. There has been so much money spent on this house. Lawnmowers, grass-sweepers, fertilizer, shrubbery, seed, *water*. Tons and tons and tons and tons of water, spewing forth from the sprinklers every day, straight up in a Rockefeller Plaza-type spray from the soaker hoses along the driveway, out like a fan and back and forth from the yellow ones that sit in the back—and finally, yes, the ultimate, the Godsend: The Melnor Travelling Sprinkler! You lay out a route for it that will cover the whole front lawn, and you turn on the water, and—gasp! amazing!— it moves! It follows this route! It travels along that hose-map for the whole afternoon, and turns itself off when it comes to the end. So there's none of this stuff about having to run out and move the sprinkler, none of this getting hot and wet and all that. It's tricky; it's like a clock, you know, it's like you can't see it moving at any particular second but if you go away and come back in fifteen minutes it's in a new place. But I saw it move. I saw it. I sat on the front porch once and glued my eyes to the wheels, and I caught it! It was weird, though. It was sort of . . . alive. Moving by itself like that.

These machines, these machines. My father is amassing an army of machines in the garage to conquer the world. We have a lawnmower for cutting the front, one for the back, and one for around the bushes. We have a snowblower (which doesn't work), and he is talking about buying a machine that blows leaves into piles, or a vacuum that could suck them out of the planters! No more of that horrible picking, picking, sitting, sitting, boring, boring, boring . . . it could just sssssssuckem out with all those churning horsepowers. I used to be against the idea of riding lawnmowers; I thought they were flabby American sissy contraptions, like the families riding by in their Sunday cars. But when I think of all the work that these machines can do instead of you—yeah. Bring on the motors. This old guy next door has gotten onto the idea of mowing up all his fallen leaves with the lawnmower. I don't know why. Maybe he thinks it fertilizes the lawn. My father says it's because he's a lazy son of a bitch. My father hates the guy because his dog pissed on our shrubs once and they all died. Sometimes you see the two of them working in the yards on opposite sides of the border, not looking at each other or speaking, just standing there raking, my father hating him because he works too little and him hating my father because he works too much. It's like that; I get the idea that a lot of people can't quite understand my father sweating over the yard and the house as much as he does. But they would understand if they could be around at about 7 P.M. on some summer weekend evening, after the lawn has been freshly cut and looks like a green carpet; with the Melnor Travelling Sprinkler moving motionlessly across it; as he sits on the front porch, drinking a brown bottle of Horlacher beer, with my mother; as cars slow down to gaze when they go by. Sometimes men stop and come up and ask my father just how he did this or that to the yard. Or when we have company and he takes the guests on "The Grand Tour" (he calls it that) through the immaculately furnished and decorated house, which has been called "The Versailles of Glenwood Drive" by neighbors. But whenever I am caught with my feet on a table or my hands against the wallpaper—oh God. "GET YOUR FEET OFF THAT TABLE! GET YOUR HANDS OFF THE WALLPAPER, IT LEAVES SPOTS! YEAH, YOU'D UNDERSTAND IF YOU'D SPENT THE KIND OF MONEY WE'VE SPENT ON THIS HOUSE! JUST WAIT UNTIL YOU HAVE A HOUSE, BOY, I CAN'T WAIT, YOU'LL SEE!"

So you see, then, how I never want a house. I never want a lawn. I never want any of this furniture that you can't touch because it cost too much, I never want any house that's so beautiful you can't have a basketball back-board on it, I never want any more of this life where you work all week and then you work all weekend, I never want any more of this work, work, work, WORK! Why can't it be raining, or windy? Why is Sunday always a beautiful day?

"Son. You'd better be getting up, now. Your father is already outside. I'll call you in to breakfast when it's ready."

Shit.

WHY WE ARE IN VIETNAM

by
Daniel
Peters

Originally published as
"Yale Basketball in
Dallas," in *The New
Journal,* Vol. Two,
number ten, April 27,
1969.

PART I

Heritage and a Skirmish

Daniel Peters glanced around the Dallas airport, not taking much of it in, merely feeling glad to be on the ground once more. The trip from West Virginia had been a long one, and the jet had encountered some turbulence as it approached Dallas. He couldn't figure it out: the sky had been blue and the sun had been shining; there seemed to be no explanation for the jarring their stomachs had received. It was as if the placid blue was only a civilized veneer over treacherous winds that raged underneath.

Most of the team had survived the buffeting with few ill effects: after the flight to West Virginia only a hurricane could seem worse, Bill Kosturko, the third-string center, was sick again. He was beginning to be known as Blap-bag Bill, and his fame was spreading from airline to airline.

In the cab on the way to the hotel, Daniel examined the passing scenery with the curiosity he usually invested in towns seen for the first time. He noted the large amounts and variety of shrubbery that crowded the yards of the homes they passed. He wondered what kinds of beasts and reptiles inhabited those homegrown jungles. Probably spitting cobras and big old Dallas mountain lions. He was startled by the numerous Lincolns and Cadillacs that stood like pagan idols in the midst of the shiny-slick magnolia jungles. The notion of Texas wealth impressed itself on his mind as the dim remembrance of some youthful incredulity.

The Hilton Inn was a huge, vertical edifice surrounded by foliage that seemed like a modern re-creation of the Alamo. The doors were huge bronze slabs that looked like the gates of Troy, and the hallways were spacious and high. Dan could almost see a handful of Texans stomping Santa Anna's ass right there in the vestibule.

There was time to work out in the gym before dinner, and Dan liked the feel of the floor. He was looking forward to tomorrow's game with real eagerness, mostly due to the strangeness which the whole affair held for him. He found it amusing that an Ivy League team should be playing basketball in Texas. It was something he had never pictured in his mind as happening to him; for in his youth his speculations had been confined to the Midwest and, more recently, to the East. That's what made the visit so strange, for the area and its people were entirely outside the range of his conjectures and expectations. He guessed that he'd just have to see first and form opinions afterward.

He went back to his room after dinner, not feeling energetic enough to go flicking with some of the others. He decided to read some more Henry James. He'd finished *Daisy Miller* on the plane, and had two more novels to finish for the exam, which would take place a week after the team returned from the trip. He had read *The Ambassadors* in another course, and it had caused him to reevaluate all his ideas on tradition and civilization. He had decided that perhaps there was something worthwhile in standards of taste and conduct. For too long, he had been caught up in the type of American cultural hubris epitomized by the Daisy Miller character. There were no ethics except those that suited the moment: this, he knew now, was a moral cop-out, for his innocence was not really profound enough to permit such absolute freedom. Money, power, and youth could not make up for abominable breaches of humanity and decency; he was not so far beyond good and evil as he would have liked to have been. Someday, he thought, Americans will learn that they cannot act any way they please and still expect to be revered and liked. He winced inwardly at the self-criticism implied in this thought.

The evening was uneventful, until Dan and his roommate, John Gahan, heard the return of Thatcher Shellaby, the team captain. They met him in the hall with the usual curses and animal cries that pass for friendly greetings with jocks, and he answered in kind. The noise attracted some kids who were having a party down the hall. Obviously bored with their own fun, they ventured out to see what they might have been missing.

At first there were only three guys, all sandy-haired fellows with beers in their hands. Thatcher explained that he and his teammates weren't having a party and politely declined the proffered invitation to theirs. The conversation turned to small talk, and it was eventually revealed that they were from the state university whose team Yale was to play the next night. The atmosphere seemed to change subtly when Dan replied that he and his fellows were from Yale.

There was the usual "Oh, wow, I'm impressed" attitude that Yale's name elicited from so many. Ordinarily, this was followed either by genuine interest or a little game of "do you know?" But the Texans' reaction was different, probably due to the fact that their girls had arrived. The situation had been growing increasingly uncomfortable once the preliminary amenities had been exchanged, and now vague threats were murmured and the air filled with hostility. Dan, John, and Thatcher could feel the danger but were not able to fathom the reason for its existence.

Thatcher decided to cool it by announcing that he was going to bed. One of the Texans replied, "You'd better get in that room, faggot."

Taken aback, Dan stared at the speaker. The boy was well dressed, wearing a white shirt, flannels, and a tie, and his hair was neatly combed. He was leaning against the wall, obviously somewhat drunk, and he uttered the threat quietly and coldly.

In a manner quite unbecoming jocks, Dan and John retreated to their room and ignored the subsequent knock, presumably a last attempt to stir up the fight which the Texans seemed so ardently to desire. The Texans had all been neat and had seemed rather quiet. No one had even raised a voice. Then why the threat of violence? That such quick belligerence could be manifest with such utter civility was unsettling. It was like being bitten by a smiling baby: unforseen, unexpected, and painful.

What kind of people invited you to a party in one breath and threatened you in the next? That kind of invitation didn't leave the guest much room for choice or negotiation. It was like forcing your way of doing things onto someone else against his will. To reject the fun offered on their terms was to insult them and bring injury on yourself. It seemed, all in all, a rather self-righteous form of amiability.

Dan went to bed puzzling over this, and was a long time finding peace in sleep. He dreamed of smiling Texans bombing the Eiffel Tower.

PART II

More Heritage

The previous evening's confrontation was only a dim memory, more like a dream, when John and Dan went to breakfast. Dan read the Dallas *Morning News* while they waited for their food. He turned to the editorial page, for he often found editorials amusing. He wasn't disappointed.

One editorial was basically concerned with Texas fruitcake, supposedly the best in the world. That honor you can have, thought Dan magnanimously. The editorial then continued to say that, as a matter of fact, all Texas food was better than that produced elsewhere. It ended by saying that *all* kinds of goods were better if Texan, and it urged one to buy Texan, for "what Texas makes, makes Texas."

The letters to the editor were even more edifying. The first complained of a cartoon which the correspondent thought reflected favorably upon the Chicago protesters. He lamented this situation, saying that the Chicago police should be lauded for their just and heroic fulfillment of duty. The editor informed the gentleman that he had misinterpreted the cartoon, which in reality had knocked the protesters and praised the police. Dan wondered at both the possible ambiguity of the cartoon and the wit of the interpreter, but decided neither mattered as long as everyone agreed on law and order.

The second letter was an attack on the "utopian Left." It stated that the Left's nonviolent premises (no manifesto was quoted) were hypocritical because the Left continued to support such "violent" measures as the War on Poverty and Urban Renewal. This flagrant inconsistency made it "clear" to the writer that the Left was unfit to "rule" (as opposed to govern?). Dan's cynicism was prodded by every word. Ah yes, he thought, reminders that there are ghettos do such unmitigated violence to my tender sensibilities. Such reminders must be silenced, with clubs if necessary.

Dan had encountered this kind of thinking before. His first acquaintance with it, through the Chicago *Tribune,* had thoroughly shocked him, but since then he had become hardened to conservative rhetoric. He paid his bill and returned to the hotel, where an expedition to explore Dallas was forming.

Dan joined Thatcher, Bill Kosturko, Jack Langer, and Larry Schwarz in a cab. On the way into town he noticed a sign advertising a conservative newspaper owned by a Texas millionaire, one of the world's wealthiest men. He knew a little about the owner's reactionary politics, how he had had veto power over George Wallace's choice of a running mate and had vetoed Happy Chandler because of his leniency on the racial question: Jackie Robinson had entered the major leagues while Chandler was commissioner of baseball.

They unloaded themselves from the cab in front of Neiman-Marcus, Texas' famous department store. It seemed no different from other department stores, until they began to check price tags. They examined a three-foot-high statue—$1750. It was an antique from Hong Kong. A small vase went for the same price. The silverware department carried gold table settings; one candlestick holder cost $600. Dan was disgusted with himself because he knew he was gawking, and the fifteen-dollar ties and sixty-dollar slacks finally drove him from the store. As he left he passed Pearl Bailey's personal Christmas tree, unguarded in a glass case behind a counter, laden with $35,000 worth of pearls.

The idea of a department store for millionaires struck him as the most tasteless example of capitalistic excess he had ever seen. It seemed to say that material wealth was an elemental and necessary facet of everyday life. It also said something about the community that supported it; for what kind of people flaunted their extravagance so openly? Did the ability to support the expense of such extravagance make them feel somehow superior to other people? In the cab on the way back, Dan came to the conclusion that someone's priorities were fantastically screwed up.

While waiting for the pregame training meal in his room, Dan tried to make further headway in James. He was beginning to doze off when Thatcher and a girl Thatcher had met in Neiman-Marcus knocked on the door.

Thatch introduced her as a Sarah Lawrence girl whom he knew from Yale. She was home for Christmas, and she was going to find them some entertainment in Dallas. Rob Jackson and Glenn DeChabert also came in and asked her where there might be some action.

She began to call nightclubs, explaining that the best entertainment was to be had in "Africa." Incredulous, they asked if "Africa" was Dallas' black district. She replied that it was. Glenn, a Black himself, remarked, "Damn. In Los Angeles, they call it Watts; in New York, they call it Harlem; but in Dallas they call it Africa. Shit."

Being typical products of adolescent-repressive America, they asked the usual question: "Will they card us in Africa?" She replied, quite calmly, that the only thing they ever checked for was a gun. Was her calm demeanor meant to add shock value to her statement? He remembered that Gahan had said earlier that there had been

eighteen shooting deaths in the state over the weekend.
Dan was inclined to believe her.

At the training meal later, Thatch described what he
had seen at her house that afternoon: two maids, a Rolls
Royce, a Porsche, a Lincoln. Dan tried to connect this af-
fluence with her calm acceptance (expectation?) of violence. Did that much money give one a grand indifference
to injury, or was it the power-masculinity thing again? His
speculations were cut short by the coach explaining the
two-one-two zone, and he decided it was time to start thinking about basketball.

PART III

Americans at War

During the pregame warmup there were a few catcalls concerning Dan's sideburns and Jackson's and Whiston's hair,
but they had become inured to this long ago. The Dallas
papers had prepared the fans for the Yale players' appearance (and the players for the verbal abuse) by remarking
that "Morgan led Yale in scoring and Whiston in haircuts."

The band struck up "Old Time Religion" as Yale's
opponents took the court to warm up. This favorite was
alternated with "Dixie" and "The Eyes of Texas." Dan had
his first inkling of what they were up against: as far as he
knew, the "Star-Spangled Banner" had not been played, but
he figured that the substitutes would do well enough for
those present. It was the feeling that counted.

Yale opened in a zone defense and promptly ran into
problems. State was able to penetrate far enough inside to
suck the Yale guards in, and then they were pitching out

for the open jump shot. They were hitting well enough from the outside to take a ten-point lead by half time. The first half had been a ragged one for Yale, with too many errors and not enough defense. It had also been a rough half, for the opposition was rebounding fiercely and the referees were unusually lenient on body contact.

The second half promised to be even rougher. Yale was going out in a man-to-man defense, with pressure at half court, and they were determined to hit the boards harder. Yale's coach reminded his players that their opponents considered this game a breeze, a warmup for the games coming up. They didn't expect a real contest from an Ivy League team; it was taken for granted that intellectuals from the East couldn't compete physically with Texas athletes. That figured, Dan thought ruefully. As a kid, you were a pansy if you preferred books to baseball and a sissy if you weren't prepared to play rough or dirty, or to lie in order to win. Sportsmanship was a shake of the hand when the mayhem was over.

The action in the second half was fast and furious. Yale's defense tightened and their fast break began to operate effectively. The referees allowed the game to become even rougher. John Whiston, the Yale center, went in for a lay-up on the fast break and was laid out flat on his back by a State player. No foul was called. The mayhem under the boards was even more flagrant, but Yale seemed to give as much as it received.

But the tide was turning; Yale was slowly narrowing the deficit. Resting on the bench, Dan noticed that the fans became more frantic as Yale edged closer. He also noted that all the Blacks were sitting together in one section behind one of the baskets. They were mostly black girls, and they were cheering for Yale. Dan guessed that this was chiefly due to Glenn's presence on the team, for he was a very handsome fellow and seemed to attract black girls wherever he went.

The referees' decisions became more and more dubious. Every time Yale threatened to tie or pull ahead, they were charged with some infraction that nullified their effort. It was what is known as a "home job."

With Yale pressing, Rob Jackson was called for a highly questionable blocking foul, which prompted Yale's Jim Morgan to remark to the ref, "That was a ridiculous call." State got three free throws and the ball, and their lead was increased.

The initial skirmish took place as time was running out. State's forward, Sutter, exchanged words with Shellaby and then with Morgan. A small pushing match ensued, but it was quickly quelled. The crowd was yelling for some Yale blood.

With two seconds left in the game, State had put the game out of Yale's reach, but the animosity latent in the State team and in the crowd had not been vented. Shellaby was shooting a free throw, and Morgan went back in a safety position, along with State's Laimen. Laimen decided that he wanted the spot on which Morgan was standing, so he began to push Morgan out of the way. Morgan, in pushing back, grabbed Laimen's shorts, and the two started to grapple.

At this point, Glenn DeChabert stepped out onto the court and warned Laimen to lay off Morgan. Whether or not a white player would have had the same effect on the situation remains a moot point, but it was a black man who was out on the court challenging Laimen. Sutter got to DeChabert before Laimen and gave him a tremendous shove. The battle was on.

Dan was at midcourt as the entire State bench rushed at Morgan. They were hitting Yale with every man they had; even their coach got in a few licks. Dan had been in fights at games before, and they usually ended with both teams holding the combatants apart until tempers could cool. Following this theory, he grabbed the nearest State player and pulled him clear of the fray. Pinioning his arms, he said, "Okay, man, let's stay out of this; let's cool it down."

But the State player made no reply; he continued to struggle. He displayed no rage, only an eagerness to join the fight. Dan was reminded of attempts to restrain fighting dogs. He looked over at the bench and saw Larry Schwarz, a Yale substitute, swinging at three State fans. The situation was entirely out of control. The State players and fans seemed to be fighting for some reason greater than anger. With their greater physical prowess and numbers, they should have easily mopped up the Yalies, so the latter's staunch resistance only increased their anger and determination.

Dan suddenly realized the precariousness of his own situation. He was standing at midcourt holding a struggling State player, surrounded by angry fans. The fans included not only students, but also men in their thirties and older, probably men with families, surely men who considered themselves adults. The chances were looking good that he'd get his head beaten in if the scene didn't change rapidly. He realized that the role of court policeman clearly wasn't a one man job. He released the player.

Finally, the Texas Rangers began breaking up the melee, though where they had hidden themselves for so long remains a mystery to this day. Players shook hands, and fans were escorted back to their seats. Shellaby resumed his place at the free throw line. The foul was shot, and the game ended without further mishap.

Walking off the court, Dan glanced up at the balcony. A balding, bespectacled man was standing, shaking his fist angrily, shouting at him: "You come from Yale? You look like you come from Yale!" Dan wasn't quite sure he knew what that meant, but it certainly had a vitriolic ring. He was amazed that a man his father's age should become so vituperative over a game. Then again, he thought, it was not so different from the unreasoning anger his father had revealed in their arguments on Vietnam this past summer. With filial feeling, he smiled sweetly at the man and walked up the stairs to the locker room.

The locker room was a cacophony of excited voices: a mixture of indignation, bewilderment, and hurt feelings. Glenn sat with his head bent, tears in his eyes. Dan hadn't fully realized the deep racial overtones until he saw how Glenn was taking it. Gahan told him that the three men who had attacked Larry Schwarz had been sitting about three feet away from the Yale bench, within earshot of Paul Oliver, another black Yale player. Gahan said that the men had been loudly calling Glenn a "nigger." Glenn viewed the entire episode as a racial attack. To an extent, Dan thought, he was right. There had always been in America this elementary vindictiveness and disdain for the Indian, Negro, and Asiatic peoples, a disdain which makes a loss or concession to these people a disgraceful blow to honor and prestige. But Dan thought there was more to this than racism.

He wondered if there might not have been some moral complications present in the game situation which the State players were trying to vindicate with the fight. The help given by the referees and by their own rough play put something of a moral taint on the victory. The margin of victory had not been very large, and an analysis of the game could give the difference to these factors alone, making Yale an equally good team. It was, therefore, necessary and pragmatic to settle the contest physically: the resulting free-for-all was the final attempt to establish clear superiority.

A reporter gave Dan another hint as to the reason and peculiar nature of the fight. He was questioning Morgan on the cause of the fight, and he said that Laimen claimed "Morgan grabbed me by the balls." This conjured up immediate visions of the near fight in the hotel the night before. The game had been a real challenge to their masculinity after all, and to have to struggle so hard against lesser men was actually degrading to them. Jesus, he thought, when are these people going to give up their hold on the Old West? Will they always be proving themselves men with their fists and guns? Shit, why don't Americans grow up and realize that to be a man goes beyond the archaic notion of the two-fisted, red-blooded, hard-driving, non-intellectual man with the hyphenated sensitivity that one reads as "sub-human?" All his mind's eye could see was the vision of State's Sutter with his nostrils distended and his little pig eyes blinking and glaring, sightless with bestial rage. He'd probably make a good soldier, Dan thought; at least his hair was short.

He talked with Paul Oliver as the team walked from the gym to the hotel. Paul was a quiet Black from Alabama, and Dan decided that, this night at least, he was the bravest man in Dallas. He had stayed out of the fight, even when Glenn was attacked, and he explained why. "I've been in fights like that before. Where I come from in Alabama, people don't go out to push and shove; they go out to hurt and kill. Every fight I've ever been in was a racial one; if I had gone into that fight tonight, I would have really hurt someone."

But he hadn't joined the battle, because he preferred to do violence to his self-esteem rather than to another man. It took a lot of courage to do that, and a lot of pride and assurance in his own masculinity. Dan felt the familiar pang that always struck him when he met a peaceful man; it was admiration and frustration rolled into one ache. Why couldn't people just coexist? The hell with the label of "ridiculous idealism" and the retreat behind pragmatism; let's do what's human for a change. He left with a helpless sigh and went looking for some marijuana.

PART IV

The Advocates of War

His lungs tingled from the smoke and his head felt very light. Grass was such a pleasant, relaxing high after exerting oneself. It might not be good before a game, but afterwards it sure beat salt tablets. Unfortunately, he didn't think he could ever get the NCAA to sanction it.

Paul Harvey was on the TV, about to deliver a commentary. The commentary was in honor of the American Legion, whose memorial day or week was imminent. He spoke of the men who had fought in a "better war," of men who had fought in the trenches without gas masks, morphine, the USO, or proper equipment, and of men who had come back to face depression after exerting themselves on the battlefield. These were the men who thought America valuable enough to fight and die for it. Harvey's voice broke at this point; he was openly in tears. At a loss for words, he ended with a wave of the hand.

Dan was on the verge of nausea; such maudlin sentimentality was almost unbelievable. The American Legion was notorious for its hawkish stance on the Vietnam War, and their right-wing activities were well known. The past efforts of these men did not change the situation today. All crimes and mistakes could not be wiped out by the remembrance of good past intentions. World War I just didn't make it as a justification for a war that affected *him*. But again, he remembered he was in Dallas, where such things did go on. This made Harvey's absurdity painful rather than laughable.

The sports news contained a brief account of the brawl. It made no comment on the contest other than to say that Yale had lost. The newscaster said that Laimen had been set upon by two Yale players. This made Yale sound a lot worse than was the truth. Dan found his mind brooding over the reports of Viet Cong losses given earlier. There was a connection, he thought, but he couldn't quite put his finger on it. He gave up and returned his attention to the news.

The sports announcer was defaming the character of Don Meredith, the Dallas Cowboys' quarterback. He was interviewing a teammate of Meredith, and was feeding him damaging, leading questions: "Do you think Don will ever recover from such a public humiliation as the Cleveland game? Do you expect any major personnel changes in the near future?" The teammate fended the queries off as well as he was able, but at the end of the interview it was clear where Meredith stood in the eyes of the commu-

nity. In closing, the announcer quoted a New York reporter, who had said of Meredith: "It must be hard on a
guy when he realizes that he's one of life's losers."

Meredith had not only had a poor football game; his
team had not only lost the Eastern Division title; he had
totally disgraced himself as a man, as a human being. One
could not afford to lose in Dallas. Losers did not belong
there. Real men had to win every game, fight, and war, or
else die trying. Dan suddenly felt very claustrophobic; he
was glad they were leaving town the next morning. Right
now a drugged sleep was the best refuge from the reac-
tionaries who haunted his waking hours.

PART V

Resolution

Dan read the Dallas newspaper accounts of the game the
next morning while waiting for the cabs to the airport.
They referred to the Yale players as the "longhairs from
Yale," and carried much the same story of the game as the
newscast of the previous evening. One even credited Yale
with winning the fight, though not the game. Such equa-
nimity is truly touching, Dan thought.

He thought about the millionaires, the game, and
Dallas in general as the cab sped toward Dallas Interna-
tional Airport. Dallas was the town in which Kennedy had
been assassinated; it was Lyndon Johnson territory; it was
the only major city to go for Richard Nixon. Dan knew
that Dallas country was one place where he could never
live. They wouldn't tolerate his kind here. It was an America to which he couldn't belong, one which he couldn't

allow himself to join. The attitudes it represented, the battles it fought, and the way it fought them, were things he could not support. He knew that the only way of life for him was one of resistance to the Dallas consciousness, which he knew existed everywhere in America, usually in forms more subtle than those of Dallas. The irrationality and danger, however, were the same.

As Dan headed up the hallway toward the plane, he stopped for his last look at the Dallas airport. He raised his finger defiantly in salute, and as he headed into the plane, he muttered under his breath, "Hot damn, Vietnam."

THIS
IS
THE "REAL WORLD"?

John S.
Rolander

Repeat after me: I do solemnly swear"

　　　—"I, John Rolander, do solemnly swear"

　　　—"That I will support and defend the Constitution and laws of the United States of America"

　　　—"That I will support and defend the Constitution and laws of the United States of America"

　　　—"Against all its enemies foreign and domestic."

　　　—"Against all its enemies foreign and domestic."

　　　—"So help me God."

　　　—"So help me God."

The matronly clerk had been swearing in new postal employees for the past twenty years, but she still put her glasses on and read the oath from a card she held subtly in her palm. She put the card down and picked up a sheet marked "Summer Substitute Carriers Assignments." Then, speaking in an official-sounding voice, she said, "Mr. Rolander, you have been assigned to the Woodland Station at Fourth Avenue and Elm Street. Tomorrow morning at five o'clock report directly to your supervisor there."

"Thank you very much, ma'am."

"Oh, Mr. Rolander, here's your badge. Wear it at all times with your uniform."

"Thank you, ma'am."

"Good-bye."

"Good-bye, ma'am."

Three dollars and fifty cents an hour is good pay for just walking around delivering mail. I knew it would be a drag, but with twenty percent of the city unemployed it was good to have a job at all.

The alarm began to ring at 4:00 my first morning. By 4:15 I had shut it off. I stumbled over to the closet. I put on my regulation blue post office shirt with my regulation blue-grey post office pants, grabbed my regulation grey post office sweater and went into the bathroom. While trying to ignore the reflection of my beardless face in the mirror, I combed my hair neatly behind my ears. Breakfast consisted of a piece of toast and a glass of orange juice.

From my apartment in the north end of Seattle to the Woodland Station was a twenty-minute drive. I arrived an appropriate ten minutes early, finally awake enough to begin to function properly. At one end of the large room where each mail carrier sorted the mail for his route I saw a desk with a name plate on it: Supervisor—Oscar Mitchell. Sitting behind the desk was a short man of slight build; black horn-rimmed glasses dominated his face and his crew cut was neatly trimmed and radically short.

"Excuse me, sir. My name is John Rolander. I was told to report to you this morning."

"You're the new summer sub?"

"Yes, I am."

Mitchell began searching through one of his files. He looked at me briefly and spoke quickly, evidently trying to impress me with his efficiency: "Read this and sign it." It was official Post Office Department Form No. 3047-R, concerning life insurance. I signed it and handed it back to him.

"Have you ever worked for the Post Office before?"

"No, sir."

"You're a college student?"

"Yes, I am."

"University of Washington?"

"No, I go to Yale."

"You'll have to get a haircut." Mitchell wasn't looking at me. I hoped he wasn't serious.

"But at the employment office they seemed to think it was short enough."

As if he hadn't heard me, Mitchell continued to shuffle papers, without looking up. Eventually he responded: "I don't give a damn what they told you at the employment office. I'm the supervisor at this station. I'll expect to see you tomorrow with your hair cut." He looked up at me momentarily; I said nothing. "I don't have anything for you to do today. Be here tomorrow at five." Mitchell resumed his search through his files.

As I was leaving, the regular carriers were gathering around the time clock. They varied in age from early thirties to late sixties, most of them closer to sixty. It was 4:57, but they were not supposed to begin work until 5:00, so they all stood there waiting for the three minutes to pass.

"Hey, Wilbur," one of them said to another in a loud voice, "Did ya hear about the guy that had a job workin for the railroad in Thailand?"

"Can't say as I did."

"He was layin ties! Get it?"

The men laughed uproariously. For the next few minutes they stood around repeating the joke over to each other, saying, "Yeah, that's a good one." At 5:00 they clocked in and proceeded to the coffee machine to "start the day off right."

I walked out to my car and found the parking lot almost full. The cars were mostly early 1960 models of Fords and Chevrolets, all of them proudly displaying decals or bumper stickers with the American flag and slogans of the "America: Love it or Leave it" variety. The pick-up truck parked next to my car carried a sign in the back window: "If you hate pigs, next time you're in trouble call

on a hippy!" The lack of peace symbols was quite evident:
mine was the only one there.

It was no easier to get out of bed on my second morning. I again donned my uniform and saluted smartly at
myself in the mirror. I had cut off a full inch of my hair
the night before and couldn't help feeling somewhat naked
with that additional inch of my neck exposed. It'll grow
back by September, I consoled myself. I tried not to think
about my roommates, traveling in Europe, free.

At 4:50 I found Mr. Mitchell at his desk filling out
more official-looking P.O.D. forms. He completely finished
the one he was working on before looking up at me. As
warmly as possible I said, "Good morning, Mr. Mitchell."

"Good morning," he responded briskly. He was looking at his desk again instead of at me, but I was pleased
that he wasn't examining my haircut. "Rolander, I've got
a job for you. Nelson left today and won't be coming back
for a month, so I'm going to give you his route while he's
gone. It's number 3463." He pointed to the empty case
where I was to sort the mail for the route. "If you have any
trouble getting the mail cased up, Hank there can help
you out."

I walked over to the case, quite aware of the fact that
almost everyone in the room had been watching me. The
fellow next to me was the only black man in the room.
"Are you Hank?" I asked. He nodded. "My name's John.
It's good to meet you."

Hank smiled and offered me his hand. As we shook, I
was relieved to see the men going back to their work and
resuming talk among themselves. Hank told me that my
route was among the worst at the station. In a lowered
voice he said, "That Mitchell's a real bastard, but don't let

him give you no shit. He treats everybody like that, but we just don't pay no attention to him."

I settled down to the monotonous routine of sorting letters. Since it was my first time on the route Hank had to help me with the sorting, and I was a little late in getting out of the station; but I finished delivering the first half of the route early and got back to the station on time for lunch. Mitchell had left me a note saying that he wanted to talk to me after lunch.

I took my sack lunch into the side room where the other men were eating, found an empty corner, and sat down. Two oldtimers sitting near me were carrying on a heated discussion about the Postal Reform bill, which allowed women to be mail carriers. "It's a man's job and they know it!" said one to his spectacled and balding friend.

His friend was shaking his head. "I just can't understand it, Joe. I mean, it was bad enough when they started hirin all them darkies, but hirin women to do a man's job is goin too far."

I looked around to see if Hank was in the room. He was sitting by himself reading the paper, evidently oblivious to the others in the room. Joe continued talking: "You know, I think it's part of a conspiracy; a plot to degrade the status of the mail carrier." His friend was nodding; both were genuinely concerned. "You remember back during the depression, and during the War? Nobody was talkin about hirin any women back then. Bein a mail carrier was something to be proud of!"

"Yeah, those were the good ol days; when men were men and women were women, and you could tell the difference!"

Just then a few more men came in and sat at the

table with me. Yesterday I had seen them standing around the time clock. The joke-teller was leading the conversation. "Hey, Wilbur," he began, addressing the lanky man who had taken the seat next to me, "d'you know why there's such a big overpopulation problem in Japan?" Without waiting for Wilbur's answer he burst out, "too many elections!" He laughed louder at his own jokes than anyone else did, but we all laughed along with him. For five minutes he entertained us with jokes that vaguely recalled the Party Jokes pages of past issues of *Playboy*.

When he ran out of dirty jokes, as if they had just noticed my presence, the men began to talk with me. The questions they asked seemed directed toward verifying the fact that I was, in spite of my appearance, really a WASP who enjoyed chasing women and drinking beer. Once that was determined I was apparently admitted into their fellowship. The joke-teller, who had been directing the conversation, whispered to me confidentially, "Let me give you a word of advice, son. Most of the fellas at this station are pretty regular guys, but you better watch out for Hank. I mean, Hank's a good man, but I just don't think he's cut out for carrying mail at this station. You know what I mean? I'm not telling you what to do, but that's just a little friendly advice." He gave me a slightly exaggerated fatherly pat on the back and announced to the group that he was going outside to have a smoke. The others followed him out, leaving me by myself once again.

I decided to look for Mitchell. He wasn't at his desk, so I checked with the clerk and was told that he had received an emergency phone call and wouldn't be in for the rest of the day. Quite pleased, I finished my route and went home for the day.

The third morning, while driving to the station, I

began to feel uneasy about seeing Mitchell. I had a slightly queasy feeling in my stomach. I didn't think he could fire me just because of my hair, but Post Office regulations did specify that hair should be trimmed above the collar. I pushed my hair behind my ears and tried to slick it down a little before I went into the station.

In the mail-sorting room there was more noise than usual, and the men seemed very relaxed. I saw that Mitchell wasn't at his desk, so I went over to talk with Hank.

"How ya doin?" he asked me.

"Alright. What's going on here this morning?"

"Oh, the men's just goofin off cause Mitchell's on emergency leave for the next two weeks. I guess his ma died, or somethin like that."

"That's too bad."

Hank grinned at me and said, "Well, it is and it ain't. I mean, it's too bad his ma died, but it sure will be nice wit'out him on our back for a few weeks."

I nodded, realizing how glad I was that I wouldn't be seeing him for two weeks. Looking around the room, I caught the eye of the joke-teller for a second; he purposely looked away from me, disdainfully. I felt my cheeks flushing slightly, but Hank didn't notice. He suggested that I go clock in: "Ain't no use in standin aroun this place and not gettin paid for it." I agreed.

The assistant supervisor didn't seem to know what he was doing or particularly care what we were doing, so the men took advantage of him constantly. They claimed that the mail was much heavier than usual and worked an hour or two of overtime almost every day. Most of the time I avoided serious conversations with the other carriers, and was satisfied to do my route and go home early.

As I got more familiar with the route, I finished increasingly early, which pleased me because I wanted to get home to see my girl friend, who worked nights. The assistant supervisor was also pleased, because fewer man-hours made his efficiency rate higher. After seven days on the route I was finishing in about six hours instead of the eight hours the route was supposed to take.

In a number of short conversations before work I came to know the joke-teller better. His name was Arnie Jorgenson and he, like me, was of Scandinavian descent. We had attended the same high school, too, although thirty years apart. He never made any further references to Hank or my overt friendliness with him, but I could still sense his antagonism about it.

The Friday before Mitchell was to return I wanted to get home particularly early so I could leave for a camping trip that weekend; I was getting ready to go home while some of the men were still eating lunch. I recognized Arnie's voice calling me from the lunch room, "Hey, Rolander! What do you think you're doing?"

"Getting ready to go home."

"You're finished already?"

"Yeah. I had to finish early, because I'm going camping this weekend."

I couldn't quite hear what was being said inside the lunchroom, but someone called out, "Rolander, get in here. We want to talk to you a minute."

I walked into the room. Only Arnie, Wilbur, and two others were there. They stared at me as if I were a defendant on trial and they were each prosecuting attorneys. Wilbur said, "Say, John, we've noticed that you've been finishing pretty early lately. Think you're pretty fast, do ya? Or do ya think maybe Mitchell will give you a raise when he comes back?"

THIS IS THE "REAL WORLD"?

"No. It's just that I have a girl friend who works nights, you know, and I like to see her." I looked toward Arnie for support but he was looking the other way.

One of the men glanced at me condescendingly and said, "Mr. Rolander probably doesn't know that Civil Service sets the wages, and brown-nosing the boss doesn't do no good."

I again said that I only wanted to see my girl friend. Then Arnie entered the conversation: "Look, Rolander," he began in his fatherly manner, "you're being a fool. That route of Nelson's is supposed to take eight hours to carry, and he's been trying to get it cut for a year now. What do you think happens when the supervisor here tells the inspector that the summer sub carried it in six hours? Nelson gets screwed, that's what happens. Now quit being a fool. You can take it easy, kill a few hours and get paid some overtime. Then you're happy and we're happy. Okay?"

"Yeah. Thanks for telling me," I said, still sensing hostility from the other men.

Wilbur wasn't through with me quite yet, though. He warned me, "When you get on my route next month I don't want anybody gettin their mail early. You understand?"

I nodded.

Arnie tried to soften the hostility. "I think he understands now," he said to them. Then to me, "Go ahead home, and tell your girl friend you won't be seeing her so early next week."

"Yeah, okay." I was relieved to have the examination over. "Good-bye," I said, smiling weakly, and left the room.

I finished getting my things put away and went out to my car. The other men had left, but Arnie was waiting for me in the parking lot. He seemed to be waiting for me to say something, so I told him that I really hadn't known

I was making myself so unpopular at the station.

Arnie patted me on the back and said, "That's alright. It takes a while to understand how the Post Office works. You see, most of these guys have been working for the Post Office for most of their lives and you know what they've gotten back? Nothing. Nothing at all. You bust ass for the goddamn Post Office and do twice the work in half the time, and you know what you get? Half the pay! There's no sense in killing yourself off for nothing, is there? If you don't do all the work they give you they can't fire you. So why should anybody work hard? It's not just a summer job for us, you know, this is all we've got. You see what I mean?"

"Yeah, I do." I liked Arnie, but I was still bothered by the pressure I felt from him about Hank.

Arnie suddenly grinned at me and asked, "Do you know how virginity is like a balloon?"

"No, tell me."

"One prick and it's all over!" he said gleefully, slapping me on the back. We both laughed loudly, and then Arnie left, wishing me a good weekend.

"Thanks, Arnie," I said. "See you on Monday."

Monday morning I had a hangover. My head ached and I felt like I was looking at everything through a fishbowl. By the time I had washed and dressed it was twenty minutes of six, so I knew I would be late on Mitchell's first day back. Not only that, but I hadn't shaved all weekend, and I'd forgotten to have my Post Office shirt washed and ironed. I left without breakfast and drove twenty miles an hour over the limit, still arriving five minutes late.

I made a point of not looking toward Mitchell's desk the whole time I sorted my mail. I left the station to begin delivering the mail on time without Mitchell saying any-

thing to me, and worked at a leisurely pace so I had half
my route left at lunch time. Feeling much better by then,
I came back to the station to eat my lunch, but on my
locker Mitchell had left a note saying that he wanted to
talk to me after lunch.

I expected a confrontation with Mitchell, so while I
ate I worked out a few speeches in defense of myself. I ate
quickly and went into the men's room to make myself look
as presentable as possible. I tucked in my shirt tails, spit-
polished my loafers, washed my face and hands, and
combed my hair behind my ears. This time Mitchell was
sitting at his desk, obviously waiting for me.

I approached him politely. "It's good to have you back,
Mr. Mitchell. I'm sorry about your mother."

"Thank you," he said in the brisk, business-like manner that I had become accustomed to expect from him.
"Rolander," he began, regarding me intently, "I was under
the impression that before I left we agreed that you would
have a haircut."

"Yes, we did, and I did have one." His hard stare continued. "I guess it's grown back in the two weeks you've
been gone," I added.

"Look, Rolander," he said, looking away, "let's not
play games. When I said a haircut, I meant a haircut. I
don't expect you to wear it as short as mine, but I'm telling
you seriously that I will not have anyone with hair as long
as yours delivering mail for me."

Knowing that it probably would not succeed, I decided
to appeal to him personally anyway. "Mr. Mitchell," I said
somewhat jokingly, "just what is it that you don't like about
long hair?"

Mitchell clenched his fists and his cheeks flushed.
"Long hair," he said, his voice surprisingly restrained, "to

me represents everything that's wrong with our American society today. Your grandfather and his generation and your father and his generation fought and died to make our country what it is today, and now you and your hippie friends are saying it's no good. And what do you have to offer that's any better? You smoke your marijuana, burn flags, dress like bums, wear your hair long, refuse to fight for your country, and go to colleges run by the communists." He paused for a second and stared at me. I said nothing. "And Yale is no exception, either. I read about the riots there last month. And your president, Booster, or whatever his name is, is a commie, too. Everybody knows that the Black Panthers are trying to destroy our society. Only a communist could support an organization like that. It's time people like you left college and found out what it's like to live in the real world."

"But, Mr. Mitchell—"

"Don't interrupt me! I know what I'm talking about. All these riots, I know they're started by outside agitators who are all communists and they aren't part of the universities at all. And they go to training camps in Russia and China and learn how to infiltrate into the colleges, and brainwash our college kids into believing all their propaganda. And they get into the high schools, too. I know because I've got a daughter in high school and she tells me it's true. And let me tell you that she doesn't go around with any of those long-haired guys; in fact, if I ever saw her with anyone who looked like you, she'd never hear the end of it, and she knows it!"

Mitchell stopped to take a deep breath. I still didn't say anything. "Have I answered your question?" he asked me.

"Yes, you have," I replied politely.

"Fine, go finish your route then."

Out on my route, I thought of a dozen brilliant responses I could have made to Mitchell. Then I tried to decide whether it was worth not having my hair cut as a matter of principle. I felt I had bent enough to the Establishment by shaving off my beard, but I decided to check with the ACLU before determining how adamant I could be about my principles and my rights.

Because of the late start I had made on the second half of my route, I finished late, and found no one except Mitchell at the station when I returned. I ignored him while I was putting my things away, but just before I left he called over to me. "Rolander, could you come over here for a minute?" Very pretentiously I clocked out, and then walked over to him.

"Yes?" I said, annoyed by the fact that he was shuffling papers around in his file again, evidently disregarding me.

"Rolander," he said looking up at me with a trace of a smile on his face, "I spoke with the personnel office this afternoon, and it seems they want to transfer you. Evidently the Roosevelt Station in the North End needs a sub, so I told them we could spare one." He tried to look at me pleasantly. "It's probably nearer to your home, too, isn't it?"

"Yes, it is," I told him, trying to show no emotion. Mitchell looked at me earnestly and said, "Rolander, I want you to know that this isn't because of our little discussion about your hair. I checked your record and you've done a fine job here. I want you to know that, as a carrier," he paused meaningfully, "I have a lot of respect for you."

Evidently I was expected to feel that that was the

supreme compliment from him: even if I was a bum or a commie, Mitchell still respected me "as a carrier!"

"Thank you, sir," I replied.

Tuesday morning I arrived at the Roosevelt Station an appropriate ten minutes early. I found the supervisor and introduced myself to him.

"You're the new summer sub?" he inquired.

"Yes, I am."

"Are you a college student?"

"Yes, I am."

"You'll have to get a haircut."

MY FRIEND CHUCK

by
Donald D.
Lindley

This past summer I worked for the Club for Boys in a small Eastern city. Because of my experience—I had worked there the previous summer—I was placed in charge of the summer group guidance program. My job was to set up a summer program, hire five competent group leaders, and recruit from eight to twelve boys for each group. Every two weeks we would start again with sixty new boys. After getting each group started, I would handle all administrative details, staff problems, and any "problem" boys.

Although only meager funds were available, I was able to hire a fairly good staff. One of the girls hired, Mary Dewey, especially impressed me. She had considerable experience, but more important was her obvious commitment to social work. To her the summer was to be more than "just a job."

After establishing a program with my staff, which consisted of four college-student group leaders and four high-school-student assistant leaders, I focused my attention on recruiting boys. This was no problem, for "Fun Club," as we had named the program, sold itself to the boys. Near the end of the first week, I received a telephone call from Mr. Ralph Jones, a case worker for the State Department of Social Health and Welfare. He said he had a boy who he thought would benefit from the Fun Club program. Mr. Jones made an appointment to come in the following Monday.

Mr. Jones was a typical caseworker. His commitment was genuine, but he was so overworked that it was impossible for him to do his best for any of "his" kids. Mr. Jones was about forty years old; he knew that he was out of touch with many of the boys he worked with. He was somewhat a "square," or "not cool," but at least he knew it. After some informal conversation, Jones began to tell me about the boy he wanted to enroll in the program. The boy was twelve years old and had a bad family background. (I was to find out just how bad later.) He had a record, to quote Mr. Jones, "longer than most three-time losers." He had spent a year at the state correction home and had just been released from psychiatric care. He was returning home to see if he could get through the summer without getting into trouble at home or with the police. If this summer trial was successful, he would be allowed to go to a city public school in the fall.

At first I was a little overwhelmed; I didn't know if either my staff or I could deal with a boy with such problems. Jones assured me that, in his professional opinion, we were qualified, and he added that he thought that Mary Dewey might be a good group leader for the boy. After discussing the problem with both Mary and my supervisor, I agreed to take the boy. The rest of the week I spent planning, recruiting, and wondering what would actually happen on the first day, the next Monday.

Monday came all too soon, and as I drove to the club, I wished I had one more day to prepare for the Fun Club program. Mary was in my office making coffee when I arrived. She was very emotional and excited and apprehensive about the day ahead of us. As we were talking of the plans, we were informed by the general secretary that Mr. Jones was on his way up to see me and was accompanied by a boy.

Mr. Jones introduced us to Chuck Moyer. The child was a model of courtesy and control. His innocent blue eyes and friendly smile made me wonder how such a charming-looking boy had gotten into so much trouble. Mr.

Jones was obviously pleased at the way Chuck reacted to us and he left with some hope for a successful summer for Chuck.

Chuck's first day was a complete disaster. He had gotten along with Mary very well, but by noon he was threatening one of the other group leaders and had been in three fights with other Fun Club members. After lunch Mary brought Chuck to my office. Here was my first "problem" boy.

The smiling friendly boy I had seen in the morning was now a sullen and defensive child. Clearly Chuck had had many rough times, and now he was expecting to get it from me. Instead of lashing into him or lecturing about cooperation, I simply suggested that we go for a walk outside the club. Chuck was visibly surprised and I wondered if he thought I was going to be easy to overrun. As we walked along, Chuck's hostility slowly disappeared and soon we were having a very pleasant conversation about sports. Chuck was obviously a bright boy, more articulate and sensitive than many of his peers. Finally I brought up Fun Club and asked Chuck what had happened. For a moment, he seemed to be putting up the defenses again, but then he said, "Oh, they just made me fight, but don't worry, I'll do better tomorrow."

I left it at that, wondering who "they" were and what the next day would be like. For the next few weeks, Chuck had nearly perfect behavior. He had won the respect of the other boys in his group and was functioning as the leader. He had also become Mary's right-hand man. She gave him the responsibilities of leading and controlling the group and his response was excellent. Mary couldn't quite believe it.

Chuck's main personal achievement was learning how to swim. When he came to Fun Club, he was afraid to get into the water, but as the weeks progressed, he had worked his way into the advanced or deep water swimming group. Most all of the boys were impressed with his achievement. It usually took most of a year to be certified for advanced swimming; Chuck had a hard time concealing his pride. Making deep water swimming at the club was a big thing. It opened the door to scuba and lifesaving instruction and was a great status symbol for the boy.

One problem came up. To get into the scuba classes and to make use of his advanced status outside the Fun Club, Chuck had to take a physical exam. During the summer, the club gave several physical exams, but these were only for boys going to overnight camp. Chuck could not afford a physical on his own and it began to look as if Chuck's main achievement was to be negated. The only possibility was getting Chuck through the camp exam. This meant dealing with the club bureaucracy and obtaining special permission. I talked to several of the executives and they all thought it would be all right. We told Chuck he could have his physical.

The examination day was cold and rainy. I drove Chuck to the health center and waited for him in the reception room. Suddenly he came charging out, crying, and screaming "Fuck you!" at everyone and everything. I tried to restrain him, but he shouted, "Let go of me, you old liar!" Mary was finally able to calm him down, and I went into the examining room to see what was going on. By this time, I was upset too.

I was confronted by a stern-faced, dumpy lady in a starched white nurse's uniform. She informed me that I was positively not allowed beyond the door and that I had better leave right now. As she ushered me out, I explained that Chuck had been given special permission to take this physical. She replied (the words still ring in my ears), "Rules are *rules*. I need written permission to allow any exceptions. We can't make exception to the rules."

I was having a hard time controlling my own temper by now, but I managed to stay calm enough to explain quietly Chuck's situation and how very important this physical could be to Chuck's successful adjustment.

As if she had not heard me, she said, "Rules are rules, young man. Now will you please leave?"

I left, feeling the rage that Chuck had expressed so vehemently moments before. I called the Club but the supervisor was not in, and "by the rules," he was the only one who could give written permission. Chuck would not have his physical.

I tried to explain things to Chuck but he lost his control again and yelled, "You're just like everybody else. You lie just like everybody else. I hate you, you liar!"

With that he ran from the building toward his home. Mary wept as I drove her back to the club. We had failed Chuck and done something we were never supposed to do —break the boy's confidence in us.

The next morning, I went to see the club director. I asked him why I wasn't given the written permission necessary for Chuck to get his physical. He replied curtly that he didn't have time to worry about one boy. From that day on, I began to realize what the club was all about.

Chuck did not come back to the Fun Club, so I called Mr. Jones to explain what had happened and notify him of Chuck's absence. Mr. Jones said he would talk to Chuck as soon as he could and suggested a meeting in his office in a couple of days. I thought this would be to explain Chuck's withdrawal from Fun Club.

I went to the meeting with downcast spirits, but when I arrived Chuck and Mr. Jones greeted me with smiles. They had worked out a new plan. Chuck would work for half a day and then spend afternoons at the club. He would no longer be in the Fun Club. Chuck left to start his job, and Jones explained how a job could benefit Chuck both financially and mentally. He felt that this would be a new and more difficult test of Chuck's ability to adjust. Chuck would spend afternoons at the club doing whatever he wished. Jones wanted me to spend one afternoon with Chuck each week, since Chuck had told him that I was his friend. I was certain that this could be arranged.

I left Jones' office with a feeling of confused happiness. Chuck must have realized what I had tried to do for him, but I couldn't be sure of this. My new relationship with him would not be easy. I would have to walk a fine line, remembering that I could not allow us to become too close. I would have to return to college in September and Chuck might feel betrayed. The hurt would be deep if we became too close. But then I could not be too distant either. Chuck needed an adult friend.

My first afternoons with Chuck were very pleasant, but we didn't really talk about anything of importance. I did make it clear to him that I would be leaving in the fall. Chuck showed surprising understanding and seemed interested in college. We went to the zoo, played catch, and went fishing.

The third afternoon, Chuck invited me to his house to see his room. I had seen run-down houses on other home visits, but never had I seen a "home" comparable to

Chuck's. It was nearly impossible for me to conceal my amazement. Dirty dishes were everywhere. Papers and trash were scattered throughout the rooms. It was clear that no one had cleaned the house for a long, long time. The furniture was dirty and worn. Most disturbing were the numerous empty Scotch and bourbon bottles scattered around and under the chairs. Chuck led me straight through this mess to his tiny room, which was really very nice and neat. It was obvious Chuck had spent a great deal of time fixing it for my visit.

The next week, I asked Chuck about his family. At first he was reluctant to talk, but then he opened up. His father, an alcoholic, died when he was eight. Chuck told me that many times his father would take him along to bars and occasionally buy him a drink. One drunken night he fell down a flight of stairs and fatally fractured his skull on concrete.

Before his father's death, Chuck's mother held the family together by working nights cleaning offices. Chuck was the only child, and she and Chuck had been close, but after the accident she became more and more discouraged and began to drink as heavily as her husband had. Chuck described summer nights when he was locked out while his mother entertained her "boyfriends."

Chuck's life turned more and more to the street, and in his confusion and loneliness, he quickly got into serious trouble. His crimes included bicycle thefts and vandalism. At the age of ten, he was caught trying to rob a house. Soon he was under psychiatric care at the state reform school for boys.

Chuck wouldn't talk about reform school and his hospitalization, but it was clear to me that he despised it and that he was deathly afraid of being sent back. It seemed whenever Chuck had any problems, Jones would threaten him with this. Chuck's only comments were, "People only got worse at that place," and, "All they tried to do was make a machine out of you." I assumed he was talking about the military discipline.

As I became aware of Chuck's hatred of the reform school, I began to see what a hopeless situation he was in. Fear motivated him to stay home, to be good. But even if he made it at home, he would have nothing. At home he was not wanted, loved, or cared for. Chuck had only a choice of the lesser of two evils, and I think he realized this.

The rest of the summer was fun for both of us. We managed to find something enjoyable to do every time, and on the rainy days we would just talk. I was getting very close to Chuck. I looked forward to our afternoons as much as he did, and parting at the end of the summer was probably more difficult for me than him.

Before leaving, I visited Jones and told him about Chuck's fear of reform school. Jones just laughed and said, "Don't tell me that he's gotten you to fall for that story." Jones didn't know Chuck at all.

Several weeks after I had returned to college, I received a letter from Jones saying that Chuck was in trouble again and that soon he would have to send him back to reform school. I sent Chuck a letter and asked him what was going on. He replied quickly saying that the only "problem" was his new girl friend: Mr. Jones didn't like her.

I wrote to Jones, and in his reply he explained that Chuck's problems were more than just having a girl friend. The girl was sixteen, and he suspected that she was introducing Chuck to drugs. Chuck's performance in school was deteriorating rapidly and he was also fighting with his mother. They were preparing to send Chuck back to the state reform school.

I called Chuck the night I received this letter from Jones. Chuck was happy to hear from me but he wouldn't discuss his problems, acting as if his home and school problems didn't exist. I advised him to explain things to his girl friend and to take things easy with her for a while. He said he couldn't tell her about his past and that I just did not understand.

Two weeks later I received a letter from Jones informing me that Chuck was back at reform school. His mother claimed she had found marijuana in his room, and this was more than enough to send him back. Jones said Chuck would be home at Thanksgiving and urged me to visit him then.

At Thanksgiving I found a different person. Chuck's face constantly showed the sullen hatred I had seen the first day of Fun Club. The girl that he had liked had dropped him and the love he needed so much had been taken away once again. He hated reform school more than ever. It seemed that he was giving up. He showed no interest in doing anything. As I was about to leave he started to cry, and asked if I couldn't get him out of the school. I said I would try, but I think we both knew nothing could be done. I tried to reach Mr. Jones, but he was on vacation.

On December 12, I received a telegram from Mr. Jones informing me that Chuck was dead. He had apparently committed suicide.

Most people involved dismissed Chuck's death as inevitable: he was mentally ill, a "born delinquent"; there wasn't much that could be done for him.

I knew this wasn't true. Certainly Chuck was confused—too many problems were thrown at him at a very early age—but he was never given a fair chance. The people and institutions that took control of Chuck's life were largely responsible for what happened to him.

All this reflects the philosophy of our society. Anyone who has trouble obeying the rules is sent to an institution. Too often such places are understaffed and rely on threats and a militaristic discipline for "reform." Once the problem person is neatly out of the way society forgets him. The close, sensitive, and deep understanding that most people need simply "costs too much." Some boys break, or reform, perhaps becoming the machines Chuck spoke of. Others don't change, and prison is their first stop after reform school. A few, like Chuck, escape in the only way they know.

ALL I WANTED WAS TO SING

by
Mary
Wilke

I taught myself how to read before I went to school. Thousands of other children have done the same thing, but my elementary school had apparently never before enrolled a literate five-year-old and didn't know exactly what to do with me. First of all, my parents were reproached for having permitted me to learn so much. The teachers told them that if I found it boring to wait for everyone else in my class to catch up with me and, therefore, turned completely against education, they would be the ones to blame. Obviously the fault was not my parents', but the school's. The program was so rigid that when they found a child who loved to do the very thing that they were teaching, my educators saw no alternative but to impose boredom on me until the margin of my head start was narrowed. Their fear that I would forever after associate learning with boredom was logical but, as it turned out, unnecessary. Boredom implies a lack of anxiety, and anxiety was not lacking in my school. What I first associated with learning was not boredom, but shame. The moment I walked into school I was considered a problem child, and knowledge was at the heart of my problem.

In first grade I was not allowed to exercise the knowledge I had acquired, but was expected to feign ignorance. For instance, though I had read, on my own, many books of the same degree of difficulty as *The Little White House* (and, I might add, a thousand times more interesting), I was not allowed to read that one until I had first read several books that were even duller and easier. The message was always: "If you show what you know, the other children will be discouraged."

At that point, giving me a challenging book would not have discouraged the other children, for we were not yet aware of the fact that education produces winners and losers, and that if someone knows more than you you're the loser. In fact, I can't think of a more natural incentive for learning how to read than seeing another child avidly reading an exciting book. However, my teacher believed in a system of competition in which the underdog feels somewhat ashamed of his rank, and this shame is supposed to motivate him to work harder. Too much shame, though, as a result of his being too far behind, would cause a child to become discouraged. My teacher's prediction—that my reading more advanced books would discourage the others —was a self-fulfilling prophecy. She taught us all to feel discouraged and ashamed when we were not Number One, or close to it.

I remember one day when we were all reading aloud from the same book. I saw the word "was," and the thought flashed through my mind that if you spelled "was" backward, you got "saw." At the time it was an exciting discovery, and I raised my hand and told the class what I had noticed. As soon as my teacher realized what I was saying, she interrupted me and said, harshly, "Mary, you'll only confuse them. They're not ready for that." I had merely expressed my excitement about what we were learning. I had had no illusions of superiority, and I had not felt that the knowledge separated me from my classmates. But my teacher, through her words and tone of voice, set me apart from and above the others, calling them "them" and telling us that I knew something which they couldn't even begin to understand (which I'm still certain was not true). It seems to me that not understanding what I had said would have humiliated no one; but my teacher's attitude probably did humiliate some children. Furthermore, she acted as though I should feel guilty for having expressed an intelligent idea, for perhaps I had confused the other kids and in some way hindered their learning.

The more blatant system of competition, which materially rewarded and punished people for their academic achievement, reinforced the already developing link between learning and pride and shame. Whereas my teacher prohibited me from "humiliating" my classmates by reading books of my level or by expressing ideas which she thought too advanced, she constantly humiliated some of them by posting our grades on progress charts and by publicly giving out gold stars.

An important distinction must be made here. In expressing an "advanced idea," my crime had been in stepping over the boundaries of the established competition. If I read a book no one else was reading, my progress record would be incomparable to that of the other children. Thus, it would fail to serve the purpose of providing incentive for my classmates. On tests the questions and answers are standard and the bounds can not be broken. Though there is a great difference between the scores of 90 and 65, the children who receive them are still in the same race, and one child's 90 can serve as a motivation for every other child. Teachers, then, justify the brandishing of achievement within the confines of the competitive structure on the grounds that it provides incentive for the other students. But the expression of any intelligence outside of this framework is considered humiliating.

I still believe, as I did in a less sophisticated way back in first grade, that this distinction is rather arbitrary. And at the time, when my teacher posted my grades and made statements implying, "Mary can do it, why can't you?", I

felt that my intelligence was being used to shame my classmates. Using my intelligence had come to mean showing
someone else up.

They solved my "problem" by making me skip second
grade. My parents didn't like the idea, but the old argument
was revived. They were told that it was their fault that I
had learned to read so early in the first place and that if I
went to second grade I'd be bored and become a rebel. I was
a far cry from a rebel, but it was a powerful argument. I'd
have to pretend I was almost two years older than I was
(I was already the youngest person in my first grade
class), and the move might intimidate my older sister, who
was just entering third grade; but my parents were assured
that these considerations were not nearly as crucial as the
possibility that I would lose my interest in learning. The
question, "Why does second grade have to be so boring that
even the teachers worry about sending children there?"
was never raised.

So I went to third grade, and I remember being worried that no one had told my teacher that I had skipped
a grade. I also was conscious of achievement; I wanted to
be sure that she would understand why I didn't know
something I might have missed. After the first day of
school as we walked past my teacher to catch the bus, I
tried to decide whether or not to tell her that I had skipped.
What caused me to hesitate was the fear that other students might overhear me. The conflict I faced was between the desire for achievement and the fear of making
other children feel inferior. After an incredible internal
debate I walked past my teacher and said nothing. But
when I got home I burst into tears, fearing that she would
not understand my ignorance.

For teachers in my elementary school, competition

and its effects superseded every other goal, including education. When a question was asked of a class, the child who answered was often set above the others as an example. However, children who knew too many answers made it hard for the teachers to test every child and discover who hadn't been paying attention. For this reason, a child who expressed too much interest and/or knowledge often met with disapproval.

The children learned these lessons, too, and we would groan whenever a child knew or cared too much about the subject at hand. This was partially because we were aware that the teacher was groaning inside. Furthermore, we groaned because knowledge had become a contest, not an end in itself. The goal was being Number One, getting grades and praise, and people who didn't get the glory naturally resented those who did. So, instead of being filled with interested and excited children thinking and talking (and shouting) about something, the classroom was filled with children worrying about competition, thinking "Who's going to win?" and "Oh, him again, I can't stand that show-off."

Seeing the disapproval in my teachers and classmates when one child talked too much in class again strengthened the shame attached to my intelligence. The displayed progress charts continued to make me intensely aware that my success was someone else's failure. And, at the same time, the voice of achievement still whispered in my ear; those gold stars hadn't been for naught. My only alternative was to continue to do well, but secretly.

I learned not to volunteer information, even when I thought that the information might interest my classmates. I began to answer questions more and more quietly, hoping that no one but the teacher would hear me. My answers were frequently bracketed by "I think . . ." or, "Maybe it's because . . . but I'm not sure." This was a far cry from my boisterous "Hey! 'Was' is 'saw' spelled backwards!" Many times I would not answer a question at all, even though the whole class was silent and the teacher was waiting for an answer I knew. I avoided the "How old are you? Ten and in seventh grade? What are you, a genius?" sequence; I told them I was twelve. And outside of class I never ever talked about anything intellectual.

I tried to hide my grades. In sixth grade a "U" in handwriting was my saving grace: when people asked, "What did you get on your report card?" I'd answer, with a groan, "Oh, I got a U." And they'd leave it at that, having compassion for the fallible. However, teachers continued to publicize grades, and every time my teacher got up to announce the name of the person with the highest grade on the last test, I trembled with fear.

These years of pretense led me to lose interest in academic subjects. Every time a topic caught my eye a tremendous conflict tore me apart. I wanted to ask questions or talk about it, but I was afraid these signs of interest would be interpreted as attempts to show up my classmates. When I came to college I became friends with several people who were studying English literature. Their conversation awakened a new interest in me; I took an English course and read literature all summer. I had read some good English literature in high school, but I had never been inspired by it—because I had learned not to let anything "academic" affect my personal life. I did the work, aced the tests, and forgot it all within a few days. I am only now beginning to be able to personally involve myself in things that could have been a great part of my life for the past several years.

I am supposed to be intelligent, yet my personality is full of characteristics which exist solely to hide my intelligence or to help me "play dumb" when I'm with other people. On a paper I wrote just last year a professor commented, *"I'm somewhat surprised. You have a fine mind, good political sensitivity, and an ability for synthesis. It is a pity to choose to hide this intelligence rather than helping to improve class discussions."* My teachers have traditionally attributed my silence in class to timidity or the fear of sounding stupid, but they have misunderstood. Several years ago I had ideas which I deliberately kept to myself. Now the ideas leave me altogether. Teachers who think I'm shy assume that my head is bursting with good ideas which I'm afraid to express. Not so. When I'm in class my head is empty. And when a casual conversation with a peer touches an intellectual subject, my mind freezes. I know, rationally, at last, that intelligence is nothing to be ashamed of, but my decision to hide my intelligence is not a rational decision. My intelligence is involuntarily stifled by a defense system I was forced to develop in order to survive my school years.

I am not saying that I've given up, that the defense system is indestructible. I have become aware of some of the causes of my intellectual inhibitions, and of what is needed to rid my mind of them. I *am* saying that I resent that an institution which theoretically exists in order to teach children how to use their intellect tried to take my intellect away from me.

Listen: When I was in first grade I loved to sing. When it was my turn I'd stand up and sing clearly and happily, thoroughly enjoying myself. My teacher declared me singing champion. In sixth grade we each had to sing "My Country 'Tis of Thee" in front of the class to try out

for chorus. I was so nervous and sang so quietly that the
music teacher made me stand right next to him and sing
in his ear. Nevertheless, I made the chorus. In ninth
grade, when we were allowed to choose whether or not to
try out for chorus, I decided against it. Timidity and the
fear of being laughed at only partly explain why I was
afraid to try out. There was something else there, something which was imposed on me, battered into me, something which finds its roots in all of my schooling: I was
afraid of singing well—the shame of success was more
than I could bear.

Why did something as innocent and joyful as the
music of small children have to be turned into a contest?
The voices should have been sources of joy, not of pride
or shame. But my first grade teacher thought that my talent should be brandished in front of my peers to inspire
them and to reward me for my talent (as if the talent
couldn't be its own reward). I was aware of the praise,
but I was also aware that my being Number One meant
that twenty other children were labelled "second-rate." My
joy became a mixture of pride and shame, and as time
went on shame overshadowed pride. In first grade I had
had no illusions of musical superiority. My teacher was
the one who wanted a champion; all I wanted was to sing.

IN SEARCH OF
COCKAIGNE

by
Scott
Stoner

Nancy and I took the elevator down to the third floor of the Morse Tower. She needed some pain pills to kill her headache and general depression, and figured she could get them from somebody on the third floor. I followed along because we were planning to go to the movies later, and I hoped going to the movies with Nancy would take my mind off how nowhere I was at the moment.

However, the third floor was stoned and generous with their dope, as usual. Nancy soon forgot her depression in the smoke and the inane comments and the laughter. My mind was too uptight to forget itself in this group of friends, lolling about in their stoned, thoughtless joy.

Not that they were forgetting that kids their age were getting their guts blown out in Asia while Richard Nixon gave speeches complimenting the courage of the University of Texas football team in going after a two-point conversion in their 15–14 win over Arkansas. Hell, Texas was behind 14–0 and went for the two-pointer on their first touchdown, which they didn't score until the fourth quarter. It wasn't courage, it was the obvious thing to do. Anyway, how many fucking football games have been decided because the coach decides to go for the two points rather than be called a pussy? You can bet that plenty have been. The coach either wins the game and is a hero or loses but is still a hero to the American public. He wins either way if he goes for the win and loses either way going for the tie; no alumnus cries for the scalp of a coach that goes for a victory and doesn't make it—it shows that he's got balls, the alumni've got balls, the whole damn school's got balls. No one wants a pussy tie. Not in America. That's how coaches make decisions. It's such an easy out. Victory with honor.

The third floor never forgets such shit: it just wasn't into a political, social, or any other kind of life thing that night. It was that sort of a mindless group happening, where everybody is together and laughs and does his vegetable impression. Nobody moves or thinks. The room is their world. They just sit there like mindless vegetables, and refuse to decide something as basic as whether or not to go to a movie. You get the feeling that if you were some sort of animal, an antelope maybe, you could bound among them nibbling an ear here and a hair there, eating your fill while they sat there in their stoned stupor. Of course, if you could be something really big, like a lion or something, you could go trampling in among them and not even acknowledge their existence. You wouldn't really need them and could crush them or let them be, whatever your mood, or maybe stalk something bigger, like the antelope jumping around nervously in the corner and making its living off these vegetables, and yet smart enough to be aware that something a little bigger and tougher is after it.

And what would the paranoia of the vegetable be if he knew what was coming off? Anyway, I'm not so sure he didn't. I remember the paranoia I felt at Woodstock, the same paranoia Abbie Hoffman felt and wrote about in *Woodstock Nation.* I was sitting there on a hillside with about 400,000 other freaks and tripping my head off on Saturday night and some group had just finished—it might have been Canned Heat, I'm not sure. But the time went by and no group had started playing again and I knew it didn't take *that* long to set up a new group. Over the loudspeakers some fool was babbling about some kind of trouble they were having in an incomprehensible electronics jargon that I knew wasn't real, and then someone started rapping politics and shit. And someone said that the green acid was bad stuff, and so was the dark blue. It came over the speakers, so it was *official*. Shit, then I knew what had happened. They had passed out weird acid and maybe loaded the water and food with something too, and all those military helicopters and spotlights, well, there was your answer. Richard Nixon or the MC5 or someone like that, maybe communists, had got us all on this big farm, had zonked us, and now it was gonna come. Maybe a couple of divisions waited out of sight over the hill; or maybe they would just drop the bomb and say the hell with it. Were we just the bad boys in *Pinocchio* who ran away from home to the land of candy and games and then grew into donkeys and our cries turned into brays? Walt Disney did *Pinocchio*. Where would my education be without Walt Disney?

But the Grateful Dead started playing and I knew things were all right. All I had to do then was walk around a little bit and make sure I was out of the vegetable patch, because if it was coming, the vegetables would go first.

So I sat in the doorway and looked in at the vegetables, who couldn't decide something as basic as whether or not to go to a movie. It was your typical corporate decision dilemma, where some might want to go and others would go if everyone was going and others didn't want to go at all, with a smattering of totally rational types who had to know the times of all the shows, what else was playing, what would be coming later in the week, the temperature outside and which way the wind was blowing. Meanwhile the paranoia turns to a loneliness more personal than just alienation from groups and institutions.

The last day of Thanksgiving vacation, Sunday morning, my father goes into his "I'm not the one to decide what is right or wrong for you in this life, Son, but there are a few facts of life you have yet to learn" address. Now the old man has some views that are really fascinating in their way, coming from him and all. Take life: he feels it's pretty much of a joke and we're just here for our time and then we die and we're done with it. Religion he saw as a good business or a relaxing pastime, if you can get into it, but he just preferred tennis, beer, and good times as pursuits, having had his share of religion as a boy. Nor did he plan, he once told Betty and me after downing a number of red drinks (one of his own concoctions), to take up the faith in his older days, in hopes of late pardon. Yet he is still the product of the Depression generation, so that Sunday morning sermon concerned the correlation between the way people judge you, success in life, clothes, and personal appearance.

Now I had heard this rap before, so I attempted to leave the room. This only produced one of those great confrontations in which he gets some things off his chest and invites me to do the same. While I'm declining the offer in comes my mother wanting to know about drugs and grass and what kind of stuff I've been up to back at Yale. In the meantime I'm thinking about Betty, who is the kind of girl who unhooks herself from you before you unhook yourself from her, a cause of acute personal depression anyone who has ever been burned can understand.

Shit, when you start feeling bad, it's an irreversible process. The best thing to do is just lean back and let yourself feel bad, if you can't find a way out of it. Just let your rational, unemotional side smile and admit defeat and lean back while your emotional side takes over. It's good for personal feelings; sometimes I think there are those

who give vent to their emotions a little too publicly—
killers, rapists, Adolph Hitlers, Maos, and Ho Chi Minhs
—people that go around harming others. And Khrushchev,
who pounded that table like a little boy and was a mur-
derer too, like Stalin and Lenin and Karl Marx before him
(impressionistic history from the years of McCarthy and
Eisenhower). Wasn't it Ike who kept us out of World War
III by taking a bunch of Khrushchev insults at some sum-
mit conference? Yeah, that was the right thing to do at
the time, just like when Kennedy called the Russian-Cu-
ban bluff over those missiles—we all sweated for a while
there but he knew what he was doing, didn't he? And then
Johnson gets us so deep into Vietnam that it seems like
we'll never be out. Everybody hated him. But in twenty
years they'll probably love him too. The Great Society. The
New Frontier. Peace with Honor. Return to Normalcy,
the New Deal, a chicken in every pot, the Great Leap Forward, heil mein führer, love Big Brother, take a little bit
of soma and forget you're a Beta or Delta or Zebulon.
What's going on here, Mister Jones? You can talk for the
rest of your life, but you'll still have nothing to say.

Tears were kinda welling up in my eyes so I left the
third floor to take a walk, but on the stairway I see this
cat, so I sit down to be its friend. But cats are very inde-
pendent creatures, not like dogs, and they don't get involved with you unless they feel like it. I tried to pet this
cat but he just moved away, and I knew there was nothing
I could do to force him to be a friend of mine. I just sat
there feeling worse and worse, alone, and the cat was
looking at me. I guess he saw how badly I was feeling,
because the next thing I know he climbs up on me and I
rub him and scratch him behind his ears and he purrs and
licks my hand. I know he just licks my hand because it has

salt on it, but it doesn't bother me; everybody has their
ulterior motives, the ones we never find out about (or do
when it's too late). Mr. Cat and I were getting pretty tight
there, but I hear people coming and I know it's time to
move on, so I bid my friend goodbye and we wish each
other good luck. The cat decides he likes it where he is,
without too many people around to bother him, and I decide I'll go to Nancy's room for my coat and a good long
walk in the New Haven night.

I get Nancy's key and go up to her room for my coat
but before I leave I start looking out her window, just staring transfixed in some direction, I guess it was north.
Morse has those long, floor-to-ceiling windows that make
you feel as if you're standing in a picture frame, and
maybe that's how Saarinen, the architect, planned it—
Morse and Stiles were just big picture frames for a human
art exhibit, like a living Advent calendar. I strike a kind
of casual, I-don't-give-a-fuck pose as an expression of
where I am at the moment, if I can be said to be anywhere.

Right below me, five stories down, the Tower Park-
way is curving in a big semicircle around Morse, and a
Naples Pizza truck is honking its brains out trying to get
someone to pick up the pizza he ordered. Out further is
Yale Parking Lot number 73 or 117 or 3,000,000 or something—no parking 8 to 5 weekdays, 7 to 11 Saturdays, all
other times parking reserved for Yale students, alumni,
and guests. No parking in snow emergency. Violators will
be towed at owner's expense. That's what the signs for
Yale lots read all over New Haven. If they ever liberate
New Haven, they should grab those fucking parking lots,
tear up the asphalt and plant some trees there. Most of the
time the damn things just sit there, sort of big, hard black
deserts strewn with broken glass and pebbles, suffocating

the earth. And people are still cutting themselves on glass the Egyptians made thousands of years ago.

Beyond that parking lot were some small, old row houses, kind of beaten down but kept well enough so that you couldn't call them slums. And there was the Grove Street Cemetery, a huge park dotted with man-made monuments to the dead. What happened, every American back at one time wanted monuments built to him after his death —sort of the American dream, although earlier countries built monumental tombs—the pyramids, for example. But in America, Jesus Christ, every Tom, Dick, and Harry that kicks off gets some kind of little stone. That's because everybody in America is equal, although some guys get bigger, fancier stones than others. Anyway back when guys decided it would be great to have a monument on their grave, they established a precedent—that's all you have to do, establish a precedent and the thing runs almost forever, because no one has the balls to go against it—they established a precedent for putting markers on graves and leaned back with a smile, just waiting for their chance to die. I knew American death rituals were ridiculous, having read *The Loved One* and having overheard some conversation one time about *The American Way of Death*— God, I felt I was a virtual expert in the field at one time, but I know better now and realize I'm merely above average in my knowledge of the institution of death.

And beyond the cemetery stood the Kline Biology Tower, all lit up like a giant pinball machine getting racked for points all over the place, and beyond that lay Sleeping Giant Mountain (there must be an Indian legend about Sleeping Giant Mountain—if there isn't, someone ought to make one up).

Of course, over the whole thing was this big, dark

blue sky that covered everything; it always had and probably always will. The same sky was over Washington,
where all those old men sat and did nothing, and over
Syracuse, where Betty might be walking in the night or
else making love, and over Trenton, where my parents
were probably still working at the tennis center, making
money and keeping the economy alive. Actually you're in
contact with anyone in the world, because everyone walks
on the same ground and is covered by the same sky. Profound. That was the greatness of America anyway, always
motivated by the draw of the frontier, the call of the wild,
and the quest for the unknown. Wasn't it? Sure, Frederick
Jackson Turner, American history, eleventh grade, Mrs.
Updike. I had learned it in school. It was official. Nancy
came into the room.

"Well, Super, what *is* it?"

She called me Super because that was my unofficial
name at the time—Super Scott. Strange how nicknames
stick. In high school the black guys on the basketball team
started calling me Super Lew, because I was talking real
fast at practice one day and sounded like some disc jockey
named Super Lew. I knew I couldn't talk to Nancy about
what was bothering me, if it could have been explained
anyway.

"There's a pizza truck down there," I replied, and remembering that I had to go for a walk, I left. Goodbye,
Nancy.

Now New Haven was cold that Friday night—I mean
really cold, and if you didn't keep walking you'd just freeze
to the spot you were standing on in no time at all. I stuck
my hands in the old pea jacket, put up the collar, stuck
my head down and started off in the general direction of

downtown, my only objectives being to stay in motion and be aware of my surroundings. You're harder to catch when moving and more difficult to fool when aware: laws of the jungle. In front of George and Harry's Bar some car was giving off a constant, loud buzzing sound . . . it might have been warning the owner that its doors were unlocked, or its keys in the ignition, or that someone was trying to steal it. What if every inanimate object could be programmed to respond to any unwarranted tampering? What an uptight society we would have. The machines would become paranoid, the people paranoid, the flowers and trees and everything paranoid, and everyone would mind their own business and make sure that everyone else was minding theirs. Thought control, that's what we'd come to. 1984. I'd be 34 then.

The Lawrence movie house was showing *House of the Red Dragon*, billed as the "most lavish skin spectacle of all time!" If it really was, it would be banned. They always ban the latest thing to come along that tries to go a little farther than its predecessors in sex and violence as an art form. *The Amboy Dukes* was banned back in the forties, and *Lady Chatterley's Lover* and *The Story of O*, and there was *Flaming Creatures* and *I Am Curious (Yellow)*. Sooner or later the ACLU or someone takes the thing to court and proves its redeeming social value and it gets shown. Then everyone sees it or reads it and asks what the big problem was in the first place. A coed gets raped and murdered in Ann Arbor or Boston or someplace and a few people say "See, we told you so," but nobody cares too much, except that it might happen to them. The Lawrence is about a half-block back by now.

On into the night; New Haven is dotted with magical street lights that blink red-red on-and-off on one side and

yellow-yellow on-and-off on the other. A coffeehouse-eat-
ing place looks as if it's run by freaks for freaks, and right
next to it is a draft action-resistance store front. Hey, old
number 159, maybe you should look into this place! Who
was that group of draft counselors that stopped giving advice to potential inductees because after they got out on
some technicality they said the hell with it, I'm in the
clear, and this wasn't a solution to the real problem, which
was the draft itself? And they're right, of course—who's
gonna fight for a cause that doesn't affect him, unless he's
forced into it? The white man isn't going to fight the black
man's battle for him, at least not after a certain point.
Sure, it's easy for the liberal in his thirty-thousand-dollar
home to back civil rights and vote Democratic, but does
he support the police or the Panthers? And can you really
depend, in a pinch, on some white kid who passes out
leaflets for you to risk his life? You can't build a revolution on a couple of John Browns who are crazy enough to
fight someone else's cause to the death. Look where the
black got waiting for the white guys to give him equal
rights.

But Vietnam is another matter. There, we are fighting
for freedom, ours and the rest of the world's. We're fighting for Greece, Mexico, Spain, South America . . . bastions
of freedom all over the world. But everyone knows that,
159. Walk on.

I was now in a neighborhood that was mostly black.
You could tell by the row houses and low-cost apartments.
It probably wasn't all black—there might be a Puerto
Rican or Italian section nearby, if New Haven was anything like Trenton. Maybe Polish, too. There had been
some Spanish on one of the store windows back there. And
there were the little corner combination grocery, candy,

novelty, delicatessen stores that stayed open until twelve or one . . . those were the stores the old man put on his ice cream salesman. A little store in a crowded neighborhood could sell a lot of ice cream if it stayed open late at night. The people here weren't like the suburb people, who went to the supermarket once a week, spent thirty dollars, and went home to load their freezers. The folks in this neighborhood saved their money until they needed it, and if they felt like a six pack or some potato chips or ice cream twelve o'clock on a Friday night, well, they went down to the corner and bought it. That's how to make money—stay open late.

Dad had some colorful stops, and his accounts sometimes made the papers. One night there were some knifings and a couple murders at Sally's Steak House, and Carl's Market was raided for the numbers slips in the back room; and the thing was, they were good accounts. I guess they offered more than just ice cream. Excitement.

Anyway, little corner stores have enough troubles with the chain markets; to worry about survival is usually anyone's main concern—surviving with class is a secondary consideration.

Past the Connecticut Turnpike, where it heads towards Hartford, there's a lighted basketball court in the back of a school yard. A cold Friday night and nobody's playing, but back home I'd shovel the driveway and play under the porch light until my hands were red and numb. The ball would always go rolling in the snow but the fantasy of beating Trenton High on a last second thirty-foot jump shot, your forty-second point of the game—that kept you going. Maybe your next shot was an eight-foot left-handed hook that sent the Boston Celtics down to defeat in the final game of the world championship, or maybe it just gave your team a three-point lead at halftime in a regular-season tilt. When you were on you could beat any-one; anything you'd throw up would go in. If you did it long enough, someday you would know what it was like to have several thousand people cheering just for you, just once in your life. By that time you knew that fans were the least important entity in the game—the only fac-tion that really mattered were the guys in the other color uniforms who'd been doing the same thing you'd been do-ing for years. Shooting those same shots, living those same fantasies, and now wanting the real glory of winning. After a while the fun disappears and the whole regimen becomes a struggle, until you give it up and go back to where you began . . . play the game for the fun of it, and recover the lost joys of its fantasies. A three-on-three pickup game can be as important to those playing it as a state championship game, if they want it to be. The light was shining on that basket, but no one was playing there, and I kept moving.

A construction site! Some new building going up, with its half-built cinder-block walls and dirt cellars. A construction site can be almost anything to a kid. It's a mountain or a desert or a dungeon or fort surrounded by ravenous alligators. It could be the ruins of a bomb-ripped town in Italy, where the Allies are driving out the Nazis and the Fascists and saving little kids and pretty young girls. You must have seen *The Gallant Men* on television. Or Indians attacking Fort Apache in *Rin Tin Tin,* where Lt. Rip Masters, tall, dark, rugged, and he never made a mistake, still played support to a dog. Dogs have to be the all-time Number One American red-blooded beast: dogs and wonder horses. You can shove your porpoises and grizzly bears and lovable chimpanzees—I'll take a faithful dog or a wonder horse any day. I kicked an old can as I passed the construction site. America is ripping buildings down and building them up and up and down every twenty years. Planned obsolescence, that's what it is. Ha, the answer was so obvious and shitfully trite that it could almost be valid. Except they probably don't plan to make a building obsolete at a certain date—they have enough trouble keeping them from being obsolete at their date of completion. Isn't it that way with our weapons system? It's always "Well, there it is. Now back to the old drawing board." Keep on moving, not to get ahead but to keep from falling behind. You can lose the whole pack if you tear off in some other direction. If that's where you want to go.

Now let me tell you a story. It's summer, a warm summer's night; it's clear and all the stars in the sky are shining—not one is missing. Right in the middle of a big playground, call it Buttonwood Park, is a sliding board. All the land around you is flat, and about a mile off to one side of you and the sliding board are trees—nothing in between. About two hundred yards in the other direction is the road and on the other side of it, houses; little box houses all facing you. All around you is nothing but wide open space, that is, if you're on that sliding board. Miles away tower the red lights of WBUD's broadcasting antennas. No one can come near you without being seen from far off. A quiet, spacious world revolves around that sliding board.

This sliding board is different from other sliding boards—it's a house. It has three stories. Actually, it looks like a big wooden box on legs. To get to the sliding board you climb in through a hole and you're on the first story of the house—you pull yourself up through another hole and you're on the second story, where there are some windows to look out of. One more hole and you've reached the rooftop, the third story. The wall is about three feet high around the roof, so you can look around at the trees and houses and the road if you want, or just lie down on the floor and stare up at the sky and the stars.

Two people live in this house. They're a boy and a girl, both nineteen, and they climb to the roof laughing. The boy pulls some joints out of his pocket and tries to light one, but the night breezes keep putting the matches out, and while he curses the fucking night breezes he finally gets the joint lit. The boy and the girl smoke the joints, look around at the land and then at the stars and the sky, and then make love on top of that sliding board, only the sky able to see. On top of that sliding board that's standing in the center of all that emptiness, they're making love and forgetting the sky and the stars and their families and war and television and everything else. How many people really had that happen to them their nineteenth summer? Or ever? Have you? Have I?

When they finish they slide down that board and run to the swings. When you're swinging you can close your eyes and pretend that it's really not there, or look up as you lean back and watch the sky move back and forth, faster and faster. And if someone is swinging beside you, they're traveling with you and tripping alone at the same time—you're both alone and together.

Then the boy and the girl stop kicking their legs out and the swings slow and come to a stop, right back where they started. The boy and girl leave the playground, back to the car, back to their homes, back to the "real" world. The nineteenth summer ends.

.   .   .

In the New Haven night, heading for town, I passed a school with one of those modern playgrounds beside it. It was all asphalt—no trees, grass, or dirt at all—and if some kid fell down while running he'd leave half his leg scraped into the asphalt. But the playground had swings too, with seats like the strap a barber uses to sharpen his razor on, and underneath the swings there *was* dirt, not asphalt. The whole playground was new and flipped out and illuminated by spotlights from the school, just like the basketball court had been. I walked by and smiled and dreamed more pictures that ran through my mind and into the night.

Then I stopped, laughed, and said "Oh, shit," and in the next minute I was swinging on those swings, my arms wrapped around the chain of the swing and my hands in my pockets, swinging in the freezing darkness of the artificial light. Before I left I tried out all the things in that playground except for the goddamned bars, because they would be just too fucking cold, you know?

On my way back to Morse I passed an old man, obviously lonely and aching to say something to another human being, at least the way I read it. As he went by he gruffed out a hurried "Hiya, kid" and I gave him a hello. But he was right, thank God! I was Peter Pan and America was Never-Never Land, and Walt Disney turned fables into fortunes. Bokonon wrote*:

> *Be like a baby,*
> *The Bible say,*
> *So I stay like a baby*
> *To this very day.*

I kept walking in the night.

* Quote from Kurt Vonnegut, Jr., *Cat's Cradle* (New York: Dell, 1963), p. 77.

DAVID:

A FANTASY

IN

ONE ACT

by
Bill
Littlefield, Jr.

It was in the middle of his senior year at college that David DeLyons first began to notice that he was sleeping more than he ever had before. It wasn't something that he worried about at first, not something that seemed particularly serious. His normal routine continued pretty much as it always had, except that he did less work and saw fewer movies at night and missed more classes during the day as the interval between his awakening and retiring diminished. He continued to manage at least a respectable number of dates with girls who found him reasonably attractive and funny, and whom he found enormously attractive and embarrassingly vacant. He began to get along much better with his roommate, who appreciated the quiet.

But as the year progressed, David began to be a little uneasy about his growing affinity for sleep. Cracks about his hibernation began to wear a little thin as winter melted into spring. David could still counter inquiries about why he spent so much time in bed by lightly hinting that he was resting up for his bout with spring fever, but privately he began to worry. Around the middle of March he went to see a doctor, taking care to schedule the appointment for as close to the middle of the day as possible. Blood tests for everything from mononucleosis to sleeping sickness proved negative, and much to David's annoyance, the doctor mechanically prescribed plenty of liquids and lots of rest. He returned to his room, no closer to the solution than he had been before his visit to the doctor, and decided to take a nap, although sleeping on his problems hadn't proved particularly fruitful of late.

Spring in the city was lovely that year, but David saw less and less of it as each day passed. Friends stopped sitting with him at meals because he had developed the

embarrassing habit of falling asleep into his plate. Dates
became few and far between as former girl friends ceased
to be amused when David fell asleep on their shoulders at
the movies. Gradually David discovered that there were
fewer and fewer things he could still accomplish, and re-
sorting to more naps to pass the time helped to aggravate
the already vicious cycle. In short, his condition had ceased
to be a joke, and finally his roommate suggested that he
visit a psychiatrist. It didn't seem to be a particularly al-
luring idea to the increasingly apathetic David, but he fell
asleep before he could pronounce any coherent objection,
and his roommate made all the arrangements.

Still, David entered the office of Dr. Simon Singer
with certain misgivings. Obviously there was *something*
wrong with him, given the fact that he had begun to spend
as many as twenty hours of every day asleep, but still, a
psychiatrist? Here was a man who might uncover all manner of alarming evidence, who might turn David against
his childhood or family, or even against himself. Grisly
tales of endless years spent in sanitariums where one was
jolted in and out of oblivion by weird electrical devices
danced like demons into David's imagination. Good Christ!
Wasn't it possible that they might not even let him sleep?
Hell, he wasn't hurting anyone, why didn't they leave him
alone?

Fortunately the patient who immediately preceded
David came out of the office into the waiting room just
when David reached this belligerent question, for the nurse
was beginning to be a little anxious about the sleepy looking little man in the corner who kept talking to himself.
Gratefully she called out his name and informed him that
the doctor would see him now. He had almost decided to
forget the whole thing when an elderly gentleman in a

tweed jacket appeared at the door of the inner office and summoned him forward. Dr. Singer had an abundance of springy white hair, a pair of merry blue eyes which actually twinkled when he smiled at a patient, and a neat white mustache which reminded David of a friend's father who was an enormously successful stockbroker. In fact, Dr. Singer reminded David of all his friends' fathers, even his own father, who didn't look the least bit like Dr. Singer. David followed the doctor docilely into his office.

"Well, Mr. DeLyons," Dr. Singer began, after he had seated himself behind an enormous oak desk and David had accepted his offer of an armchair, "what seems to be the trouble?"

"The trouble is that I sleep a lot," David replied, noticing a little forlornly that there was no couch in the office. "About twenty hours a day recently. I don't really . . ."

"Twenty hours a day!" Dr. Singer exploded incredulously. "Twenty hours *every* day?"

"Well," David admitted, "of course, that's only been for the past few weeks. Before that it was more like eighteen and a half or nineteen hours."

"Perhaps you had better begin at the beginning," suggested the doctor. "When did you first begin to experience these extended periods of sleep? Tell me the whole story."

And so David did. He told the doctor of the mild alarm he had experienced when he began to sleep through first clocks and classes, then meals, football games and social events of all kinds, and finally the bedtime hour itself. He told of the good-natured ribbing which had turned to cruel jibes and finally uninterested avoidance as his friends had become increasingly unable to relate to anyone who could spend five-sixths of his life asleep. He related hair-raising tales of the times he had fallen asleep at the

wheel of his car before he dropped off one day just as a
toll taker on the Connecticut Turnpike was trying to give
him change. Coins had fallen from his limp hand and
scattered everywhere, and his license had been suspended.

Warming to his subject, David recalled that previ-
ously his tendency to fall asleep at any and all times had
rescued him from some pretty dull conversations, but that
recently the situation had gotten entirely out of hand.
Shamefaced, he admitted that just the other night he had
actually dropped off while making love to a girl who had
done her best to remain true to him while other friends
drifted away, but who had declared that this final insult
was the last straw.

While he had been telling his story, David had been
staring at his toes, or his knees, or his folded hands, and
he had not noticed the extraordinary effect his narrative
was having on Dr. Singer. As he reached his final revelation, however, Dr. Singer let out an astonished gasp, and
David looked up instinctively. He was amazed almost beyond belief at the transfiguration that his words had pro-
voked. Simon Singer's hair stood on end, the corners of
his mouth were wet with flecks of thick white saliva, and
his eyes fairly bulged from their sockets. Several times he
tried to speak, but he could only jab meaninglessly at David
with his hands. It was not an appearance calculated to
imbue a new patient with confidence, but Dr. Singer didn't
seem to be able to help himself.

David was on the verge of deciding to leave the office
for the second time that day, when the doctor seemed to
regain some measure of his composure and begged him
to stay. David relented and sat back down. Dr. Singer,
scarcely less unsettled than he had appeared after David's
closing remarks, darted furtive glances about the room, as

if to assure himself that he was still in his own office, and that nobody could be listening in. Finally he began speaking in an urgent whisper.

"For God's sake," he began, "don't leave now. You may be one of the few sane men left anywhere."

Now David was genuinely puzzled, for here was something that nobody had accused him of recently.

"Huh?" he inquired.

"Don't you see?" pressed Dr. Singer. "In a world in which everyone and everything has gone absolutely haywire, you've stumbled upon perhaps the only sane course of action. It's escapism refined to the ultimate degree."

"I'm not sure I follow you," returned David, who in spite of himself was beginning to be interested in what the doctor had to say.

"Why, just take a look around!" demanded Singer. "Man has reached the brink of disaster. He's poisoned his water so that he can't drink it or swim in it. He's polluted his air so that some days he can barely open his eyes in it, let alone breathe it. He's developed his capacity for self-destruction to such an extent that tiny countries with unpronounceable names, countries no larger than some of our cities, are clamoring for doomsday machines for their own protection."

"Perhaps," interjected David dubiously, "but what has all that—"

"Think of all the legs and arms and necks being shattered on the nation's highways this instant," cried Singer, hurtling on over David's interruption, "or the psyches and egos being bruised and battered in the nation's bedrooms. Great God, man's out to prove once and for all his absolute ineptitude at dealing with *any* problem, be it large or small, personal or universal, old or new, and he's doing a damn fine job of it!"

David was nearly hypnotized by Dr. Singer's intensity, but he managed to cling to his objection, and as the doctor paused for breath, he blurted: "But even if all this is true, what has it got to do with me?"

"Why, my boy," Dr. Singer practically shouted, "don't you see? You've beaten the system. You're a senior at college. You only have a few short months left in that academic womb. Something in your makeup has realized this and balked at the thought of entering a world where you'd be as responsible as the next man for the sad state we're all in. That something has regulated the metabolism of your body to dictate a beautifully simple withdrawal from all the hideous dilemmas which have so vastly overgrown man's capacity to deal with them. Great God, boy, you're home free!"

"But it isn't all like that." David was shaking his head. "I've missed a lot of other things over the last few months. What about all the *good* times I could have had?"

"Just what exactly do you feel you've missed?" challenged Dr. Singer.

David thought for a second.

"Well, girls for example. What about all the dates I've slept through or never been able to make because I was asleep?"

"Don't you dream about girls?" countered Dr. Singer. David nodded reluctantly. "And I'll bet you're much more successful with them in your dreams than you ever were before you began to sleep so much. It's all part of your body's adjustment."

"But it's not the same!" David protested.

"Of course not," agreed the doctor. "In your waking life you'd meet some girl, and she'd throw you over, or you'd get tired of her. Or she'd get pregnant and you'd have to marry her. At best you'd fall in love and get married to someone and then feel all that much worse when she contracted cancer or got maimed by an automobile." Dr. Singer threw both arms high above his head. "What man, what man on earth wins more of happiness than a seeming and after that turning away?"

David was speechless, so Dr. Singer continued.

"But dreams, there's another story. You make love to girls whose bodies and faces change before your very eyes. Sometimes you change with them. No whim is too fantastic to be indulged. The possibilities are limitless. Failure is reversible. And best of all, you never die."

"You're crazy," he muttered.

"Of course I'm crazy," Dr. Singer agreed immediately. "I don't sleep twenty hours a day. I participate in this idiotic and senseless bad joke we call life. You're the only person I know outside of an institution who's not crazy." Dr. Singer's eyes narrowed and he leaned across the desk until his nose almost touched David's. "You've got the whole problem licked," he concluded, "and you don't even know it."

Just then the intercom on Dr. Singer's desk buzzed, and he abruptly sat back down in his chair. The framed diplomas over his head began to glow softly, and a subdued whir of machinery filled the office. The wild look faded instantly from the doctor's eyes, which became sharp and clear. His tongue darted out automatically and efficiently licked the remaining flecks of foam from his lips, and his hairs crawled back into place. Dutifully he punched the button on the little mechanical box and accepted the message that his next patient had arrived.

David was almost as stunned as he had been at Dr. Singer's initial loss of composure. He couldn't believe that the quiet voice and warm handshake with which Dr. Singer bade him goodbye belonged to the madman who had insisted on bombarding him with such outrageous arguments to convince him of the good fortune of his present plight. Could this venerable old gentleman who was quietly advising him to schedule another appointment with the nurse really be the same man who had so glorified David's symptoms as an organized and successful retreat from reality?

David stepped from the office building in a daze. Outside the early April sun struggled hopelessly to burn through the grey haze that covered the city. Cars hurtled noisily along the narrow street, jockeying for position as they neared the corner, where iron bars had been used to block off the right-hand lane and jackhammers and air drills were tearing into the pavement. Tight-lipped people who all seemed to know where they were going hurried past David, and he wondered vaguely how each could hear his own private intercom so clearly above the din of the traffic and machinery.

David mulled over Dr. Singer's words all the way back to his room, where he immediately fell asleep. During his increasingly rare waking moments over the next few days, he thought about little else but the doctor's startling comments on his condition. But the more he thought about them, and about Dr. Singer's feverish contention that David was perhaps one of the few sane men left anywhere, the more he realized that this was not really a problem one could evaluate rationally. Everything was too turned around, too muddled to be approached with logic. It had nothing to do with logic. If David's continuous sleeping was sane, then all those people in the street going about their business for as many as sixteen hours every day were crazy. But there were so many of them. How did one go about convincing the entire world that it was insane? Logically?

And what about Singer himself? How did one explain his instant Jekyll and Hyde transformations? David wondered if Singer were some kind of schizophrenic himself, or whether perhaps it was part of his calculated treatment. But he'd seemed so sincere when he'd told David to try and realize just how lucky he was to have stumbled upon such a solution to life's problems.

David continued to sleep and worry alternately throughout the next week, wondering where to turn next, until one day his roommate went into his room to wake him for dinner, and David wouldn't wake up. He was breathing quietly, normally, but no amount of effort could rouse him from sleep. An ambulance was called, and David was delivered to the general hospital, where three doctors puzzled over how to determine what was wrong with him. They couldn't wake him up. They shined lights in his eyes. They stuck pins into him, and then needles filled with stimulants, but he didn't wake up. They prodded his most sensitive areas with all manner of tools and instruments. They tickled him, and he giggled in his sleep, but he didn't wake up. They made loud and unpleasant noises very near his ears, but he didn't seem to hear them, and he didn't wake up. Then they subjected him to increasingly larger jolts of electrical current until they had to stop for fear they would kill him, but they couldn't wake David up.

Finally the doctors became upset, and collectively they decided that David was in a coma.

"He must be in a coma," they reassured one another. "We can't wake him up." And even though David's temperature was normal and his pulse rate hadn't dropped, the doctors all eventually agreed that he had slipped into a coma.

"Send him upstairs to intensive care," suggested the doctor in charge, washing his hands of the matter, "and if we can't figure out anything else to do with him, maybe we can use the pump in a transplant."

Two orderlies immediately appeared to rid the doctor of the thorny problem that was David DeLyons. They were both tall and crew-cut, blond and broad-shouldered, and the muscles bulged under their starched white uniforms as they lifted David into the cart. They were working at the hospital part time because they thought that it would help get them into college. Their names were Tod and Don, and the office was always sending them each other's pay check, but they both felt very important as they wheeled David out of the elevator and into the long white corridor that led to the intensive care unit.

"What's the matter with this guy?" asked Tod, who hadn't been listening at the door on the floor below.

"He's in a coma," replied Don, who had. "They couldn't wake him up."

"Poor son of a bitch," muttered Tod, who was always muttering something like "poor son of a bitch."

"Yeah," agreed Don.

Tod looked at David's face for the first time. "Say, but I bet he was some kind of looney too."

"Why?" asked Don.

"Well, hell, just look at the smile on his face," said Tod. "He doesn't look like he had a care in a goddamn world."

"Yeah," Don agreed, "maybe he's dreamin'," and they wheeled David into intensive care.

PART

LIFE IS WHAT YOU MAKE IT

by
Robert
Walker

Just about this time a year ago today a typically straight Yalie was browsing around the jumbled masses of paper offering things for sale in Yale Station as he so often did just for the hell of it—not because he wanted something, but simply to give his day a little variety in passing the time—when one of those jumbled scraps of paper caught his eye and pulled at his soul: on that small piece of paper was an ad offering a motorcycle for sale.

Now, before you can appreciate exactly what was happening inside him you have to understand all of the connotations that lead me to call him a "typically straight guy." You see, for this guy's whole life he had always acted in a way that brought praise from the adult world that he so wanted to belong to and be accepted in. As the oldest in a large family in the farming Midwest he was always made to "set the example" for his brothers, and set an example he did. It was almost as if his whole life was going to be devoted to being that example. He grew up hard and probably a little too fast for a boy to have the time to be a boy, but he didn't mind it at all because hard work for him was a joy in itself—he loved it and was certainly happy with his life in every way.

However, upon entering junior high school he left the simple joys of rural America, because his family moved into the "big city." He took this in good stride, and soon found that he could get even more respect and praise from his peers and elders through the toil and sweat he put into academics and athletics—he was truly an athlete and a scholar.

The years went by, though, and he began to realize that life had more to offer than just the sober, mature world of adulthood. There was that all-important part of youth that he had almost completely missed—the fun and frivolity of just screwing around. In the locker room or in the halls he enjoyed listening to and telling dirty jokes, shooting the bull with the guys, and jacking around, but he could never really resign himself to relinquishing his prior role in life. It was as if others would not let him change; everyone expected him to be the jock and the "A" student. He wished to sample the wilder ways, just to see what they were like, but he didn't want to commit his life to them. They looked pretty good from where he saw it, but he just wasn't sure.

In short, our fella just wasn't satisfied with things as they were, and was mildly confused. The pleasures of academia were definitely on the slide, and though he still maintained his previous excellence, he knew he wasn't pushing himself as he had earlier. His values were changing, but he was not ready to admit that, so with the change came problems.

He was briefly saved from facing these problems by his acceptance to Yale. After all, if you go to Yale you work hard, don't you? Which made the decision to revert back to his old ways an apparent necessity. The carefree recklessness he thought he had experienced would have to be put aside, and he would surely have to buckle down again.

But slowly he began to loosen up the tight bonds of the search for the H and the HP. He stretched those bonds, yet he was unwilling to break them because he needed a stable world to use as his base of operations. From that he could branch out to taste life's sweets. His problem was to find that balance between the sane and insane, playing the jester or playing the king—to find out exactly what his real desires were. Here he knew he could not fool himself or take the easy way out, because he at least realized that it could mean unhappiness, in work or in laughter, for as long as he would live.

And then it hit him—"Cycle For Sale, needs work, cheap." Why, here was his answer to it all! Instead of piddling around doing this and that in futile attempts to capture all the freedom and recklessness he felt he had missed, why not become a wild, hell-bent-for-leather motorcyclist? Here was everything. No matter how wonderfully uninhibited anyone else appeared to be, he could now top them all simply by cruising down the street for all to see. Instead of being one of the people who envy the freedom and carefree attitudes of others, he could now reverse his role and become one of the envied, and see what it was like. It was almost a revelation. No longer would he have to wonder, no more half-hearted attempts at pure abandon; for one time in his life he would go all the way. He couldn't wait.

He didn't know it then, but he had bought that bike before he even saw it, and that was good, because he never would have bought the thing otherwise, the way it looked. It gave the appearance of already having been ridden halfway around the world and dragged the rest of the way; it was a wreck. Heck, that was nothing to him though; with a little paint and a lot of good old elbow grease he could make it look as good as new. He wanted that bike. Where, oh where, was that practical and mechanical wisdom he had obtained while growing up? Deep down inside he realized that the cycle was a pile of junk, but this was to be a totally reckless and irresponsible act. Such practical considerations were left far, far behind.

Because our boy had never even ridden a cycle before—all the more reason to buy one, right?—he went back the next day with a buddy who claimed to know a lot about bikes. The owner was there this time, and the immediate question was whether or not it would run. The owner told him to give it a kick and see. He did, and lo and behold, to the amazement of all the thing started up right there in the living room! The owner beamed, but the cycle sounded exactly like it looked—mean. But our friend wasn't scared; he was so excited he could hardly contain his emotions. Nothing, not anything he had experienced in his whole life of searching for excitement had ever been like this— it was as if he had life's ultimate high in his hands. This was living!

After a hurried moving of furniture, they got the thing outside, and then he became a little apprehensive. Now the pretense was up—he had to ride the monstrosity. Watching the owner pull wheelies in the first three gears didn't help in the least, but it did reinforce his belief that it was this wild cycle that he wanted, that anything tamer would have been a cop-out. But when it came time for him to try it, he let his bud test it out.

And so, in a flourish of reckless, insane, completely irrational behavior, without having any knowledge of cycles at all, he laid down money he couldn't afford to spend for a motorcycle he was scared to ride. He finally had had the balls to go out and do something big that would make everyone say, "You must have been crazy!" Which was what he had always wanted.

The first stage of his act was at an end; he'd got it. Now he had to see what it would be like. When he finally started it up, pushed his foot down and put it into gear, and let the clutch ever so slowly out, he felt the cycle come alive—and it was great! It was wonderful! It was living! The power was all he imagined. He loved it. He actually began to enjoy it for its own sake. When he took his friends out for rides he saw in them the longing he thought he alone had felt. But the effect the cycle had on others was less important to him now that the thrill of riding itself was making an impression on him.

However, he still hadn't seen how his cycle would affect his family and friends back home, and because of that the bike was still a symbol and not completely an item to be enjoyed. He just couldn't wait to see what they'd say when they saw it, and for spring vacation he packed it into the trunk of his car and headed home. He had it all arranged: Once he got there he pulled directly into a garage, where he and his brother immediately began to put the pieces together. Having completed that he called home to tell them he was almost there, and then went out, started it up, and hurried home—only a few blocks away.

As luck would have it, his dad was just walking out the front door as he arrived, and with engine screaming he shot out of the night and up the driveway and pulled to a halt right next to his dad, and asked, "What do you think of it?"

His father, laughing, replied, "Son, you've lost your mind."

It was now complete. He and everybody else knew that he had not ended his youth without having done something completely ridiculous.

Having sampled his parents' world he could not totally commit himself to its demands for conformity without knowing what the other world was like; yet the more he played with it the more he knew that he would never make it only in the other world of total freedom. He loved all of life too much to give any of it up, and so he began to blend the two ways together in his own way, until at last he had a combination of the two within which he could totally fulfill all of his desires.

He no longer needed the cycle to prove anything to himself or others, because he no longer felt that need, and being no longer a tool, the cycle became more and more enjoyable. He loved to take it off the beaten path and explore, for riding was now enjoyed for what it was and not for what it represented to others. The important thing was that the pressure was no longer there. He could now enjoy life as he wanted; having made that one move he was surprised to find how easily he now could deal with decisions clouded by custom or the "You shouldn't do that" type of thinking. His life became his and his alone—the decisions and all the opportunities have become his to enjoy as he truly wants to. It's just that feeling of being free. . . .

AN ENCOUNTER

by
Leigh
Crystal

Being a loner is not such an easy thing. I'm lonesome a lot. Yet I can't be with people with whom I don't communicate. When I can talk with somebody, I really appreciate it, because that kind of opportunity doesn't come too often. I've known some strange people, and sometimes I've been lucky enough to get beneath their strangeness to learn who they are and what makes them the people they are.

I expected the summer at the Cape to be like my usual solitary existence. Lying alone on the beach, walking barefoot in the evening when the tide was out, climbing rocks on cooler days, maybe even writing some philosophy or poetry. That would have been pleasant and satisfying. I didn't want life to be too stressful. I felt a strong need to be away from the high-pressure academic community, to be free from all the alienating tasks that prevented me from learning about myself. The summer seemed the time to get into myself, to get myself back together again.

A few days after my arrival, as I was getting used to the warm weather and peaceful days, I began to feel lonesome again. But I knew I couldn't join the crowds of flirtatious girls and muscular boys populating most of the beach. I knew too many compulsive groupies, people constantly drawn to groups not for the others in them but for the security they provide. Then, early one evening, as I was strolling toward the large rock where I usually went to collect my thoughts, I spotted and was suddenly drawn toward a boy who didn't strike me as the groupie type. He was wearing a white T-shirt and a pair of faded cut-offs, and he was sitting near the ice cream truck reading e. e. cummings. I sensed that he didn't mind sitting by himself. His eyes weren't watching to see who might be gazing in his direction. I had a sudden urge to know him. Defying

my usual shyness, I sat down next to him. I had a feeling
that my gesture would be accepted.

Our first conversation consisted of the usual trivia:
where we were from, where we went to school, what our
majors were. We both came from schools the rest of the
country considered academically superior, yet both of us
were down on academic rigor and disillusioned by the type
of educations we were receiving.

A week or so later I learned that Bill and I would both
be working part-time in the local crafts store, one that sold
jewelry, belts, and pottery made by the summer residents
at the Cape. I didn't particularly like to wait on the tourists,
but I did enjoy the atmosphere of the shop, and it seemed
like a tolerable way to support myself for a while. When
I learned that Bill would also be there, I was a little excited;
I was attracted to Bill in that irrational way that made
being with him exciting, and yet we could get to know each
other slowly. I preferred to get to know people that way, at
a natural rate. We'd see what happened.

I had planned to use the summer to straighten out
my head, but questions kept coming up, questions that I
should have been able to handle and couldn't. For instance,
Bill suggested that we could get an apartment together
near the shop, but I felt too uptight for an arrangement
like that. At that time I had known him for two weeks,
hardly at all, and I had no idea what he expected from
me. I didn't know if he meant simply sharing a place or
something more involved. I had to turn him down. I
wanted pressures kept to a minimum and a place to call
my own.

One weekend he left on short notice, and I surmised
that he had a girlfriend he hadn't told me about. I really
didn't care that much, and I wasn't going to pine about it.

Not worrying was one of my rules. Anyway, I hadn't really
seen Bill enough to miss him when he was away; he read
a lot and didn't talk too much when other people were
around. Other people thought he was shy and unsure of
himself; I later learned that was not the situation at all.

During breaks from work, Bill and I would sit together
in the shade. At first we had little to talk about except work
and school, and I felt unsophisticated and clumsy. I'm
blowing it again, I thought; this guy might even be interested in me, and I can't talk to him. But I don't think he
noticed. Bill was an English major, and he knew his subject well. He remembered plots in excruciating detail, and
would talk continuously in reply to a single question; I was
satisfied to let him take over.

Before long we had worked out a comfortable schedule of working and being together. I felt a few pangs of
uncertainty as I watched other girls try to gain Bill's attention. He seemed to be playing it cool; he didn't seem
ready to make a choice this early in the summer. I was
determined not to play the usual games to win his affection, and within a short time, as I had hoped, Bill and I
were enjoying each other's company, discussing our days,
and easing each other's frustrations.

I was beginning to feel happier and more self-confi-
dent than I had felt in a long time. The situation was working delightfully well. Our relationship had developed with
a minimum of pressure, and I was secure with the feeling
that Bill was as attracted to me as I was to him.

But somehow the situation didn't make enough sense
to satisfy my insecure and suspicious nature. Bill was still
leaving on the weekends. He seemed to want me around
constantly from Monday to Friday, and then he took off. I
couldn't understand his apparent attraction and even need

for me; he wanted me, but he didn't want me. I could rationalize the situation: I had boyfriends at school whom I liked but wasn't attracted to sexually. Maybe he did have a girlfriend elsewhere. I was too shy to attempt a seduction, and I also knew that it would be best for us to remain friends for the rest of the summer. Still, there were times, like the evening we drank and played cards by the bay, really fun evenings, during which I'd begin to feel loose and affectionate, when he wouldn't even come near me. In a way I felt used; maybe it was the old insecurity creeping back, but it seemed that he took as much as he wanted when he wanted it and then disappeared when the impulse struck, leaving me behind to wonder. Oh, he was clearly mine more than he was anybody else's, but somehow that wasn't enough. I tolerated an incredible amount of ambiguity because I liked him so much, but I continued to be frustrated and confused. Shouldn't he explain his erratic behavior, instead of leading me on? My pride made me think of all kinds of improbable explanations, but I also questioned myself and the value of my company.

Finally my intolerance for ambiguity won. To me it seemed as if I had started a fight; but Bill didn't call it a fight. He said that he was used to people responding emotionally instead of rationally to his argumentative statements, and that he didn't consider it a fight if two people made sense when they challenged each other. That was a compliment for me, I guess. But finally I challenged his behavior, initially not in terms of his relationship to me but on general grounds, attacking the way he criticized other people. Eventually I got around to specifics: he was so particular, and he seemed to be running away from me at times. How could I know that he didn't criticize me as much as everybody else, and that he didn't think I was merely the best thing around from Monday and Friday, at which time he went in search of better company?

He told me the truth, and I know that he told me out of kindness, so that I would understand that he did like me very much. But he was different, he said: he was homosexual, and when he took off it was to be with his friends.

My reactions are hard to describe. I realized that I was being taken into his deepest confidence, and I thanked him, and a lot of questions suddenly made sense. It might seem that the whole situation was obvious, but it wasn't. I had thought of it before, but why suspect an unbelievable solution when there are so many plausible ones within your own realm of experience? Yet, here it was, starkly confronting me. I couldn't quite believe it was happening, and at the same time I felt that I should have been less naive and sensed it before. Still, I couldn't quite believe that my random thought was being transformed into a hard and inescapable reality.

Bill and I stayed up late that night, talking more than we had ever really talked before. I wanted very much to kiss him good night, simply as a gesture to communicate my thanks, but the act seemed more inappropriate than ever. When I went to bed I had no idea what the next day would be like. I felt only that I had become a part of a strange and unusual experience.

To this day, I have found no one with a similar relationship, and that makes sense. I only became so involved because I was unaware beforehand what the limitations of my involvement were. Few people would actually cultivate such a relationship if they knew from the beginning that it would be unsatisfying and limiting. But by the time I became aware of my situation I was already involved. I fancied myself in love. I certainly liked this person and still wanted to be with him. And I knew that the end of the summer would mean the end of our relationship, so I stuck by. Eventually I realized how lucky I was: there would be no problem of how to view our relationship when I left, no strain of wondering if it would last. I left behind a very close friend, knowing no reason why he wouldn't always be my friend.

But at first I didn't believe it. I had had such great hopes for redoing myself; I hadn't counted on getting into such a heavy situation. Having focused almost exclusively on Bill, having been thrilled that I had finally found someone so much like me, and having smoothly and easily developed a comfortable relationship with him, I suddenly found it was not so easy and comfortable after all. It was weird and perverted and upsetting.

Externally things didn't change much, but internally I found myself confronted with a very difficult situation: the anger, pride, and defensiveness I had used to protect myself from Bill's apparent desertions had no place anymore. Bill reassured me that he liked me as much as anyone he knew. The ambivalence I had felt—caring mixed with frustration at his desertions—dissolved, and I was left with the caring. And the inevitability that this relationship could never be what I wanted, and the fact that it was no one's fault but nature's.

Our involvement had developed easily. We liked each other very much and never stopped having things to talk about. After having spent so much time coming to grips with my own sexuality, I was finally responding the way I'd always wanted—and now the desires were inappropriate, could not be gratified, and practically had to be denied. For a while the Secret (and it *was* a secret, because I knew that things were not as they appeared to everyone else)

became the predominant thought in my mind, blown out
of proportion. But I knew, all the while that I was hurting,
that it was going to turn into a positive experience; that if
only I could work through the hurt and be willing to feel
the caring, I could grow in a way I had not envisioned; that
I could learn to feel love without expectation or obligation;
that I could learn about a part of society from which I had
been carefully sheltered; and that I could learn, once and
for all, that there is no strength in being alone if there was
no happiness in being alone with my strength.

I don't think my inner turmoil was betrayed by my
actions. I wanted above all to appear calm, because I did
not want Bill to think that I might reject him for his "difference." My initial feelings of fright seemed to come from
my own personal hang-ups, as well as from a cultural
prejudice I hardly knew I had. The fact was, however, that
not only did I not want Bill to feel rejected, but I did not
want to reject him. I knew that I still wanted to be a part
of his life, in one way or another. If I could not make my
earlier fantasy a reality, then I would find a new reality.
The real things, I learned, may be less than dreams, but
they are still better than dreams, because only in real life
is gratification and pleasure truly believable and appreciated.

I must have appeared accepting, because Bill began
to talk to me, not just about his ideas, but also about his
experiences, his life, his wants, his hopes. At first I told
myself that I was certainly receiving an "educational" experience, but I knew it was more than that. I realized that
there must have been few people with whom Bill had felt
the freedom to be open. So many times his "cool" depended
on his hiding his secret, and those other times when he
could be open about his secret were times when he had

to be closed about the feelings and the needs. I heard about his early homosexual experiences and the uncertainty that surrounded them, the strange feelings of attraction that began as far back as grammar school and the gradual realization that they would not go away, were not a phase of life but a way of life that was just beginning. The difficulties in learning the ropes—how to go to the bars, how to find lovers, how to cover for yourself when necessary—were mingled with stories of delightful entertainment, of the discovery of a way of having fun, of associating with people who, once together with their own kind, let many kinds of inhibitions go, people who went swimming in the nude in beautiful coves at sunrise, people who gave fantastic parties and lived a life based on today because they could not trust in tomorrow. Underneath it all I sensed not only a personal struggle to find meaning, but a universal one, a struggle that pervades people of all kinds who try to learn to do the best they can with what they are.

I began to share more of myself, my real self, with him. I had no fear of rejection. If only we could all lose our fear of being rejected by other people, we could all be much more open and much closer to each other. The basic human process is the same for all people, though we may meet our desires in different ways. Loving is loving whether you are gay or straight. The hope of anticipated union is the same; and the desire for fulfillment is universal. People are people; despite apparent differences, the similarities are always greater, and even if two people cannot sustain each other indefinitely, there is always something that one person can give to another to help him through a moment of loneliness, to help him feel that he is less alone, and to help him realize that he is worthwhile and that, if not now, then someday he will find happiness.

Somewhat ashamedly, I began to realize the extent to which I had internalized society's rejections of the homosexual. After all, my involvement with one appeared to me as an unfortunate, unhappy situation. I considered it upsetting, contrary to my pursuit of inner security and increased interpersonal happiness. When the light began to dawn, the simple fact was that there was absolutely nothing bad about the relationship. Its only deviant factor was Bill's sexual attraction to other guys, and the problem I had to face was not what society labeled his deviation, but my own inability to deal with it.

I discovered that it was by no means necessary to search for reasons to prove to myself that the relationship was still good. I did not have to justify its existence. The good things existed as real and natural outgrowths of two people coming together, and the very existence of our togetherness justified our relationship's being and continuing.

Soon I no longer felt sorry for myself because I desired a person who could never desire me with equal passion. There was no rejection, only the simple reality that nature had arranged an impossibility, and it was only for one time. I began to gain insight into Bill's plight and some compassion for his frustration. Hopefully I would find fuller companionship elsewhere, and maybe soon, but where could Bill go to find his complement, his equal, someone with whom he could share his life? The number of sensitive, intellectually brilliant, and gay men cannot be great, and I knew that Bill, like myself, would not settle for an inadequate substitute. The common denominators between him and his friends consisted mainly of a mutual liking for liquor, dancing, bars, and sleeping together. The more I came to know Bill, the more apparent his sense of near-futility became; the drinking and dancing and sex were fun, but they were all taking place in order for him to find a lover—a loved one who would return his love— and it hadn't been and wasn't going to be easy.

In the middle of the summer I watched Bill develop a crush on a young artist who came to the Cape. I wasn't jealous at all. I realized that for him that invigorating process was beautifully analogous to what takes place in me when I encounter a person who excites my mind and my body. To be or even to imagine oneself in love brings a new sense of life into oneself and one's activities, and the exhilaration and guarded hope in Bill were delightful to watch. I regretted that I could not help him establish this relationship, and I discovered that I wanted very much for him to have the things that would make him happy. I could not have him, and I was accepting that, but I would have done anything in my power to increase his happiness.

I began to learn the inner strength that comes with the ability to let go, and I began to discover that, although I wanted Bill's company on the weekends, I was com- pletely willing to have him leave me, and in fact I ear- nestly hoped that on any particular weekend he might find happiness or at least hope. I knew that I could not give him the happiness that he both wanted and deserved, and, wishing his permanent happiness more than my own tem- porary security, I found that my love enabled me to let him go.

I believe I even began to appreciate another human being for the very fact that he existed, to see him as he was, to feel no desire to change him for my own benefit, to respect him for what he was and for the ways in which he accepted himself.

The relationship was not all beautiful. At times I could hardly make sense of what was in my head. My thoughts were mostly questions without answers. Sometimes my head would reverberate with the word "homosexual." I love him, but he's queer. Why is this happening to me? Frequently understanding seemed impossible. Yet maybe that was why the relationship came to seem so worthwhile, because love emerged from hurt and loneliness, because understanding emerged from what first appeared as perversion and suffocation.

When I said goodbye to the beaches and my favorite rock at the end of the summer, I knew that the two months had been a strange, moving and beautiful experience. I had come apart a bit more than I wanted to, but I had come together a lot more than I'd expected. I knew, too, that it was time to move on. I'll always be somewhat of a loner; but from now on, knowing that there was once a friend who loved me for what I am, I think I'll be less alone.

METAMORPHOSIS

by
Charles A.
Pidano, Jr.

When I was at home this past Christmas, a friend of mine, who had dropped out of the Class of 1970 at Yale, called me up. He was working for The Cambridge Institute, a private organization studying sociological and economic problems of urban dwellers, especially of working-class whites, and he asked if I would come in for an interview concerning the changes undergone by a son of working-class parents who goes to Yale. During the interview I found myself talking about American Studies 36a and about what I referred to as "the Reichian synthesis" of what's happening in America, because the course expressed in general terms many of the particular experiences and insights which I have had during the last three and one-half years and which have greatly changed my views of society and of what is important to me.

When I arrived at Yale I found myself in a dilemma not unlike that of Alexander Portnoy. Coming from a working-class family that, though not poverty-stricken, never had any money to waste, I had thought that success and happiness meant a split-level home, two cars, and a trip to the Caribbean every winter. These feelings had been instilled in me not by my parents, but by the picture of the "good life" conveyed through television, movies, magazines, etc. And just as Portnoy saw that being Assistant Commissioner for Human Affairs was not as fulfilling as he had thought it would be, so I began to have experiences which indicated that what I was working towards might not be satisfying and worthwhile after all.

I started out majoring in engineering. "Get a BS in science, preferably engineering," my guidance counselors had told me, "then get an MBA, and you can name your own starting salary." I soon found, however, that I was enjoying my two humanities courses much more than my technical ones. Science courses and laboratories seemed to be about the least relevant thing that was going on at Yale. But it was not easy to overcome my belief in the job-value of a scientific education. First I switched my major to Administrative Sciences, then to Mathematics, then to Economics, and finally, after two years, I got out of technical subjects altogether and started really enjoying my education.

Many other people have gone the same route. A friend with the same background as mine started out as an Engineering major at Tufts, switched to Physics, transferred to Berkeley and switched to Math, and finally moved into a commune, changed his major to English, and is now planning to do graduate work in that field. (His father, upon learning of the switch to English, replied, "What do you want to waste your time with that for? What kind of jobs can English majors get?" I was lucky. I never got that grief from my parents.) Yet I know many other students who are still majoring in engineering and science for the same reasons that I was, and hate it. They will probably be poor scientists, and unhappy, unfulfilled people.

But I hadn't made much of a change myself. I had decided that I didn't want to study and work at something which I didn't enjoy, but I was still heading towards my upper-middle-class nirvana. I figured I'd major in something I liked, go on to Business School, and by the time I was thirty-five be making thirty thousand dollars a year, instead of fifty thousand.

The summer after sophomore year I had a job which gave me two further revelations about the society in which I hoped to make a successful place for myself. I saw what happens to people who work in bureaucracies, and I

learned about the repressive function of law in the corporate state. I was a "junior clerk" in the Records Section
of the State Department of Probation. I worked in a large
room in which were kept records of anyone who had ever
been arrested for anything in the state. Except for four
other college students who were there for the summer,
almost all the rest of the thirty-odd people who worked in
the Records room were middle-aged women.

Most of them were not just middle-aged in the physical sense, but also in the sense of having lost animation,
of having fallen into a deep rut in life. Many had always
been single. Some who had married were already widows,
and their children were almost all married and living far
from their parents. Almost all of them had been working
in this one room at their one job for at least ten years.
Several had been there over thirty years. It took me about
two weeks to learn to work at the files; the other jobs were
hardly more difficult. I remember the college students used
to marvel that anyone could work at such a job for so
long. By the end of the summer we couldn't wait to leave.

The general effect of such jobs on these women was
what might be expected. They stretched their coffee breaks
and lunch hours as much as possible in order to make their
dull days go by faster. As they worked, or between short
spurts of work, they gossiped and argued about anything,
just to fill the time. Some would wear too much makeup
and flirt semi-seriously with the department's male bu-
reaucrats who often came out of their private offices to
break up their boring day by talking with the lower-level
employees.

These women brooked no attempt by an outsider to
make suggestions about what rules of procedure might be
better bypassed or how their job could be done better or

more quickly. I know, because soon after I started work, I made such a suggestion to one of the women, and when she disagreed with me, I tried to explain my point. She became incensed. "Imagine," she told her nearest fellow-workers, "he's been here less than a week, and he's trying to tell me about my job!" She kept talking about it for several days and was unfriendly towards me for the remainder of the summer. There was, in fact, a general hostility towards the college students. The day after the police had cracked so many heads in Chicago, several of the ladies expressed their approval, and made sure the students heard them.

There were a few women who were really pleasant, mostly ones who had not been working there for very long. But by and large the unsatisfying working life of these women made them narrow, petty, and unhappy. If this happened to people working at the middle and lower levels of organizations, wouldn't the same be true, at least to some extent, of those in the upper levels, if only because they must supervise the "alienated labor" of the employees below them? So I began to reason.

This job also gave me a chance to see the "justice" of the corporate state in action. On my coffee breaks and lunch hours, I would sit in on the proceedings of the City Police Court, which was located in the same building as the Department of Probation. There I saw the due process of law as applied by Chief Justice Samuel Woldo. This experience shattered my illusions about the "just" society in which we live.

The law seemed to work in strange ways. Prostitutes were usually given a fifty-dollar fine, which meant they had to go out and turn a few more tricks to pay it. Drunks and homosexuals were, of course, treated as criminals, and Judge Woldo often had some "humorous" remark to make about the homosexuals, such as telling the bailiff who was leading out a homosexual to "Watch yourself with him, Joe." But it was with members of the youth culture that the law and the judge showed how corrupt and repressive "justice" can become.

This summer hippies had flocked into the city, and the good citizens, of course, were appalled at the idea of these "filthy, immoral, drug-using free-loaders" entering their city. (A couple of years earlier some draft-card burners had almost been killed by a crowd of onlookers on the steps of a Federal courthouse.) The City Council immediately established a ten o'clock curfew for the Green, and in his courtroom Judge Woldo did all he could to harass and repress the young representatives of a new culture.

It soon became apparent that anytime a cop brought in a hippie for something, and the cop and the hippie had different stories of what happened, it was the cop's word that the judge took. Woldo often cut defendants short as they tried to tell their stories, and what the youngsters saw as standing on the sidewalk, or wrestling and fooling on the Green, the cops, the judge, and the law would interpret as blocking a public way or disturbing the peace. Woldo often set as a condition for suspending a questionable sentence that the defendant leave the City by the end of the week. One girl was accused by her landlady of assault in an argument about the paying of her rent. The girl denied this, but Woldo found her guilty, and when he learned she was living with her boyfriend, he suspended her sentence only on condition that they stop living together. Several hippie defendants claimed that they had been brutally treated by the police during their arrest or at the station. Woldo would hear none of this, however, saying that it had nothing to do with the case at hand, knowing that the youths had neither the time nor the money to try to prosecute the police. The cops often smiled knowingly at one another after Woldo's rulings. The older men who usually comprised the court onlookers also approved Woldo's decisions and were much amused by his derogatory remarks about long hair, dirty feet, etc.

This incensed me, sickened me, and disillusioned me. I identified with the young people (hell, my hair was getting pretty long), some of whom were students at local colleges, and I began to think that there must be something very wrong with a society that got so uptight about such harmless phenomena and which applied its laws in such an unjust fashion. Seeing films of the Democratic Convention fiasco reinforced all these feelings.

So I came back to my Yale junior year quite a bit less sure that I really did want to become part of the Establishment. My doubts were increased by the changes that were taking place in several of my friends. A friend from home had dropped out of Yale the year before, and when I saw him in New Haven that fall, he had changed greatly. While at Yale he had seemed nervous, harried, trying hard to become a real Yalie by wearing a three-piece suit and joining various organizations, but obviously not enjoying himself. Now when I saw him, his clothes were messy, his hair was long, and he seemed much happier than he had been at Yale. He was playing drums in an acid-rock group and living in a big house with a bunch of people. He seemed much more comfortable in this way of life. (I saw him again this past Christmas. He's now living in L.A., playing in a band there, and really enjoying himself.) Another friend, a very bright guy whose father is a Ph.D. and who could have gone to any college he wished, had dropped out of high school just before graduating. He had moved into an apartment in the city and also began playing in a rock group. When I saw him that Christmas, he seemed really happy and had no regrets about what he had done. Guys I knew at Yale were undergoing similar changes. Sons of wealthy families were rejecting their parents' materialistic way of life, looking for something better. All of this had its effect on me. Here were people whose opinion I respected, people I knew, not just people I read about in newspapers or magazines, who were saying that a way of life I had thought I wanted for myself was lacking in something very basic.

It was also during junior year that I read *From Here to Eternity*.* The theme which struck me the most was that of the impossibility of being a moral man in modern, institutionalized, immoral society. Robert E. Lee Prewitt tried to live by a moral code and was thus destroyed by the very institution in which he so desperately sought a place. His friend, Red, attempted to tell him this in the beginning:

> Don't you see? (Red said.) They'll always follow you around. You can't go your own way in peace, not in our time. Unless you're willing to play ball.
> Maybe back in the old days, back in the time of the pioneers, a man could do what he wanted to do, in peace. But he had the woods then, he could go off in the woods and live alone. He could live well off the woods. And if they followed him there for this or that, he could just move on. There was always more woods on up ahead. But a man can't do that now. He's got to play ball with them. He has to divide it all by two.

* James Jones (New York: Charles Scribner's Sons, 1951).

But Prew wouldn't heed this advice and kept on always trying "to decide things right."

Prew often felt the loneliness of a man, especially an honest man, in modern society: *

> Robert E. Lee Prewitt, the Twentieth Century MAN who walked upon his mother earth in an up-to-the-minute Twentieth Century PLEXIGLASS SPACE SUIT that industrial techniques produced in such munificent mass abundance that every man woman and child could have one at cost, at less than cost, at nothing actually, because our recent research has so perfected the new process that we can now make the astounding offer of an almost absolute vacuum in our newer models, this modern MAN with so much to be grateful for, with the heritage of the ages in his hands, who could hear his shoes scraping scraping against the gilt-flaking bed frame like one of the higher-priced more accurate metronomes reminding him not to get the clean sheet muddy—this creature was not even HAPPY! Just because he could not get outside his plexiglass space suit, his sanitary all-purpose-all-weather space suit, just because he was not *known,* just because he did *know,* just because he could not touch another human soul.

In the end Prewitt was destroyed because, as Warden said, "He was always a hard-head"—he couldn't compromise his principles.

What Jones said so forcefully was that the moral man who wants to be a part of modern society finds himself in a dilemma—either to become immoral and survive or to remain moral and be destroyed by a system which has no room for morality.

By the end of junior year all these experiences and ideas had convinced me that the material success I had once viewed as the way to happiness and fulfillment would

* *Ibid.*

by itself lead only in the opposite direction, to loneliness and unhappiness.

This past summer I began to see alternatives that could bring real satisfaction. I had a job which was infinitely more rewarding than the one I had had the summer before. For ten weeks I was a full-time Boy Scout leader for a troop of black and Puerto Rican New Haven kids. Just the structure of the job was great. I could put in my forty hours a week whenever I wanted to, and I could set up my own program with hardly any supervision from above. But beyond that, what I really found rewarding was working with the kids, giving of myself to them and receiving their affection and appreciation in return.

This job also showed me another source of pleasure alien to the technological corporate ladder. We went on several camping trips, but the one which had the biggest effect on me (and on the kids also, I think) was a fifty-mile hike we took in the White Mountains of New Hampshire. Carrying all our food and gear on our backs, hiking along mountain paths, not seeing a car nor a telephone pole nor a television for a week, going to bed and rising with the sun, swimming in pure, cold, flowing mountain streams, all this was a tremendously satisfying experience.

Another alternative to the corporate state syndrome is the idea of finding diversion and pleasure in ethnic cultures. I saw that to an extent this is what my parents have done. My father enjoys listening to opera or working in the garden. My mother likes cooking big meals and having relatives over to celebrate holidays. Simple pleasures, yes, but satisfying. Every ethnic group in the country has a culture which can be a source of pleasure for members who spend less time pursuing profits and promotion.

The experiences and insights I have had during the

past few years have shown me that although the corporate state produces an overabundance of food, clothing, and gadgets and diversions of all sorts, it destroys the things that are really meaningful in life—human interaction, nature, and creative culture. I have no more desire to go to business school or to work in business or industry. I plan to spend this summer with my Scouts again, and after that perhaps go into teaching or psychiatric social work. I hope to explain to people that there is a much better way of life than is presented by the corporate state (teaching offers a good opportunity for this), and I hope to show others what I mean by living a life that runs by a different set of values.

ANOTHER NIGHT

by
Robert H.
Rettew

When Tom came into the dining hall with his tray, Eric was sitting alone at a table near the back of the room, holding his head between his hands and staring straight ahead. Tom walked over and put his tray down on the opposite side of the table, facing Eric.

"You look happy tonight," he said as he sat down.

Eric looked at Tom for a moment, then dragged a smile up from somewhere, and said, "I'm just sitting here trying to decide what to do with myself tonight. I mean, it's Saturday, and I sort of feel obligated to have a good time, y'know." He looked at Tom, waiting for a suggestion.

"Well, there's a few things going on—I'm going to a dance at Fence Club . . ."

"Fuck that shit! Fence is the biggest bummer around," Eric said, a sudden expression of disgust filling his face.

Tom was nonplused. "As you like it. There is also a concert by the Symphony tonight, if you can dig it." Tom started to spoon his mashed potatoes into his mouth, indicating that he had relayed all of the information he had to offer.

"That might be cool," Eric said thoughtfully. "Do you still have that hit of acid you brought back from Boston? If so, I could get into tripping for the concert." Eric looked at Tom, hopefully.

"Sure. It's in the top drawer of my dresser. Help yourself." Tom spoke without looking up from his plate. He could be very aloof at times. Eric started to get up from the table. Tom looked up, and said, "If you're still tripping after the concert, or if you bum out on it, why don't you come over to Fence and see what the Yale experience is really all about."

"Maybe, maybe . . ." Eric was putting on his coat,

slowly, with a thoughtful expression on his face. "I might see you there," he said as he started to walk away. As he left the dining hall, he looked back at Tom, who was still sitting hunched over his tray. Eric sighed, and left.

Back in his room, Eric glanced at his watch. Seven-thirty. The concert began at eight. He walked over to Tom's dresser and opened the drawer. Underneath a pile of underwear was a small wooden box, with a peace sign carved clumsily into the top. Eric took the box out of the drawer and opened it. Inside were a plastic bag, filled with grass, and a couple of small plastic pillboxes. Eric opened one of them, poured out the contents, and looked over the assortment of speed, barbiturates, and grass seeds. He found the tab of acid, and put the rest of the pills back into the box. He walked into the bathroom and dropped the acid.

Before leaving the bathroom, Eric stood in front of the mirror, looking at himself. He stood staring into his own eyes for a long minute, then walked quickly into the bedroom and picked up his coat. Before leaving the room he made sure that he had his cigarettes, and some change. He left, locking the door, singing to himself.

Very few people had arrived at Woolsey Hall. Eric picked an upstairs seat and made himself comfortable. He started to read the program he had been given on the way into the room. As he neared the end of the first page, he felt a few tremors race up and down his spine. He glanced at his watch: quarter of eight. Shit, there must have been a little something in the acid to make him get off quick. He felt the tremors circle his body, lighting up each vein with a slight glow. Eric sat back in his chair and looked down into the auditorium.

The audience was still filtering in, finding seats, removing coats. Utter confusion of many individuals entering a concert hall before showtime, Eric thought to himself. Programs being opened, names being called out, movement of people standing, looking for seats, movement of people turning in their seats to look around, chattering voices, cigarettes being lit, buzzing movement of individuals swarming below: noise and motion.

Finally, the room is almost full, and musicians begin to walk on stage. Eric feels the heat melting through his head, gnashes his teeth, and watches the musicians find their seats and open scores of music. As they begin to tune their instruments, Eric looks at the audience. Same confusion of noise and movement. Utter confusion of an orchestra beginning to take form. Strings whining, a flute singing solitary notes, oboes squawking, various wind instruments making various farting sounds, looking for the right key, music stands being moved forward or backward, players standing, reseating themselves, leaning over to talk to one another, different notes merging with the voices of the audience high above the seats . . . Eric closes his eyes and feels the sounds seep into his body.

Sitting with eyes closed, Eric meditates on the confusion of sound around him. Someone beside him is asking someone about the solo violinist who will play tonight; someone behind him is asking someone about the football game. People all around him talking, their voices mixing with the sound of the instruments, merging with the noise from below, atonal, nonmelodic, fragmented. Eric notices that the room is beginning to quiet down a little, and opens his eyes.

The musicians are all seated, almost motionless. The audience is waiting, almost silent. The conductor walks onstage, and is greeted by a round of applause. He smiles, bows to the audience, motions to the musicians with a sweeping movement of his arm. Then he turns, facing the musicians. The room becomes quieter and quieter and quieter. The conductor raises his baton, and there is utter silence. He freezes, arm upraised, waiting. The audience is totally silent, the musicians totally attentive. All attention is focused on one person standing onstage. Eric sits, amazed by the point of the conductor's baton. It seems to be glowing with power. Eric inhales the electric atmosphere, feels all his blood quickening, melting.

Suddenly the baton falls, and the music explodes into the room. Eric feels himself jump; feels his head throb with a mighty swelling motion. The music is playing, describing a movement of water, all instruments combining to create the sea. Eric looks below, and sees the audience transformed into a heaving, swirling body of water. He watches, amazed, as the music creates the movement of waves in the room below. Suddenly, Eric sees his mind squirm out of his brain and fly into the room, searching for the music. All of the minds of all of the people are leaping out of all of the brains of the people in the room; they are flying towards the ceiling, melting into the motion of the music, becoming one mind, one sound. All of the minds of all of the musicians are squirming out of their brains, flowing out of the mouths and fingers of the musicians into their instruments, and being transformed into music, which is flowing out of the instruments and hovering around the baton of the conductor. Eric sees the conductor's baton spooning all of the music into the air, hurling it into the room, dragging the minds of the people and the musicians out of their brains, pulling them up towards the ceiling, where they merge, melting into one another, becoming One Mind, One Sound, One Dance of sound and thought.

Eric sits transfixed, transformed, glowing, melting, staring with amazement at the magic phallus which the conductor waves in his hand. Eric sees the audience become one giant female being, wrapping itself around the thrust of the music; making love and being loved, a giant act of intercourse heaving into one being high above the room. The minds of the people are all merged together into one great vulva, which is absorbing and throbbing with the music flowing from the end of the conductor's baton . . . everything is flying upwards, swirling, melting together . . .

A solo violinist stands and plays, and the Mind of the audience zooms towards that one person, and climbs aboard his music. The Mind of the audience is climbing higher and higher with the music of the violinist, absorbing it, being absorbed by it . . . the music is building and building, the Mind of Everyone is bent double, arched, reaching out all the way past the stars into the meaning of the music of one person standing onstage, and that person is staring up past the ceiling, making music fly out of his instrument . . . the strings scream, the violinist rakes his fingers across the strings in frustration, demanding more than they can possibly give . . . he is singing to the room of people and his song is melting everything together into One and he pulls his magic wand across the strings and the sound builds higher and higher   and he pulls his wand   across the instrument, demanding the very highest   and   the sound fills   the room and pulls the Mind   of the   audience   and every musician   and every thing up to   this high place   and everyone   is riding   on   the one   high note   and h ere t he re is   a m om ent e v ery one is   al l t he way   to to   the   top   and   to ge t he her   i into th ithis

on   emoment wheneveryoneis   comple tely mer   ged
into   this   one high   note   outside   the ceiling into
one ToTAL MOMent   YES   YES and then the music un-
ravels itself and the piece ends and the audience is ap-
plauding standing on its feet howling and the conductor
turns and smiles and bows and waves his baton at the violinist who is still staring up at the ceiling without any
sight in his eyes and suddenly he snaps out of his trance
and turns to the room full of people and bows and the
concert is all over and Eric is sitting in his seat waiting
for his mind to come back into his brain.

It took me a long time to get out of my seat; after the
concert ended, I was in bad shape for a while. I mean,
all I had was my own head again, and I knew it, but I kept
feeling it start to leave me again, to be with all the other
heads around me, but it couldn't do it, because all of the
people had gone back into their own heads, and were talking to each other, and putting on coats, and lighting cigarettes, and shuffling shoes, and walking all in different
directions. There was only this slight aftermath of the
mixture I had just been part of, and it was sort of wafting
above the room, getting thinner and thinner, like smoke
in a room with an open window. So I got out of my seat
and walked downstairs, and leaned up against the wall
near the entrance to the concert hall, trying to get it back
together so I could make it back over to Fence Club, where
I told Tom I'd meet him after the concert.

I was hearing everything, too—no differentiation.
Every sound was going into my head as I stood there—all
the people's voices, and their shoes making sounds on the
floor, and laughter, and programs being crumpled—every
sound was making itself felt inside my head, and since

they were all fragments, separate, not part of each other, they were messing me up for a while. So I left, and walked around outside, and waited, leaning up against the building outside, just long enough for me to be able to walk without stumbling so much.

When I had calmed down, and could hear myself think again, I started walking towards Fence Club, talking to myself about what I had just seen, and been part of, wondering what it all had meant. I kept thinking, all of those people had been so together, so together, that they had been the same person, intent on doing one thing to the utmost, something which was intense and beautiful. I kept thinking, people can do that, people can be that together, people can do that together, and can do that for other people. They can do it with music, and used to do it with religion, and they used to be able to do it with the Idea of a State, and all kinds of other things used to be able to get people to become the same person and be so together. And I kept thinking, that is the way that it really ought to be as much of the time as possible, for as many people as possible, because it meant something, and smoothed out all of the hassles and differences, and brought everyone together under this one incredible idea, which was beautiful.

These thoughts kept going around inside my head, and when I looked up I noticed that I was standing right outside Fence Club, so I started to get it together again, because Fence Club always freaks me out and I need to get a hold on my head before I go in there, especially if I'm tripping.

Tom was upstairs, in the room where the dance was, sitting in a chair, drunk so bad that he couldn't even say hello when I came up to him. So I sat down in a chair beside him and looked around the room, which was dark, and stank of smoke and booze. There were a few people standing around, talking to each other, and a few people sitting around the edges of the room, slumped in chairs, and on the sofas. A few of them were kissing, or rubbing each other. I looked at the stage, and saw a lot of heavy equipment, meaning that there was a loud band—obviously taking a break—which had a drummer with two bass drums, and an organist, and a bass with a huge bass amp, and a lead guitar with a huge lead amp. I was still tripping pretty heavily, although not as heavily as I had been at the concert, and I sat there, waiting for the band to come back and play, thinking about rock music.

I just let my mind *flow*, and I got thinking about rock music, and how I'd seen it pull people together in the same way that the concert had, except maybe better, since rock music sometimes pulls people's heads and their bodies together totally, so that they're doing this tribal thing, and dancing, and touching, all absorbed into this organic thing, part of a moving, breathing whole. So I was sitting there, thinking, when the band came back into the room, and began to tune up their instruments, and the people were starting to come back in, and stand around, talking, and waiting for the music to start again. I sat back and watched, waiting for it to happen again. My whole body was still glowing, and the acid melt kept seeping through me, so I felt hot, and molten, and good, and ready for a total experience.

The band took a long time to tune, and the drummer was making a lot of rim shots, real loud, while the lead guitar played loud single notes, and the bassist just fucked around on his strings, going up and down, waiting for the organist to find the stops for the next song. And the people on the floor were standing around restless and drunk and smoking and talking, waiting for the music to start again. I started to feel a little strange, watching all this, partly because although most of the people were talking, no one seemed to be listening to anyone else, or to be very interested in whatever the person talking to him was saying, and the people in the band all seemed to have these incredibly smug, bored looks on their faces. I leaned back a little farther in my chair.

Suddenly these huge bright lights exploded into the room, and the music began a splitsecond later, real loud, and the lights began to flicker, going on and off real fast, they were strobes, and the people on the floor were dancing, looking like figures in a real old movie, because of the way that strobes break everything up into fragments. I was rocked back pretty far into my chair, scared shit for a second by that first explosion of light, and as I tried to see the people dancing, I saw that there was some kind of haze in the room, which was getting thicker and thicker, and I looked around to see what was going on, and saw this little black box on stage, some sort of fog machine, which was vomiting all of this fog into the room, covering everything in this misty haze, and the strobes were going like mad. There were eight or ten of them and the people were twitching inbetween the flashes like ghosts or something all wrapped up in the fog and the music was so loud I couldn't see straight, the guitar was too loud and out of tune and separate from the piano which was just banging away and the drummer was pounding like hell making a lot of noise and the people on the floor were all jumping up and down inside the fog and lightspurts and I was sitting there getting more and more freaked out, trying to see what was happening and not being able to because of

the fog and the music and the light inside my head that
kept exploding so I got up and stumbled out of the room
and fell down the stairs and rushed outside and leaned up
against the wall and started to take a lot of deep breaths.

As I was leaning there, I heard a voice pretty close
beside me say, "Have a little too much to drink?" So I
turned, and saw this short square man all dressed in
black with black hair and a greasy face and a little silver
pin in his short collar smiling at me with broken teeth. So
I said yeah, I guess so, since I never go around telling
strangers I'm tripping, mostly for my own protection. And
I said that I had come outside because I felt a little sick,
because I had breathed in a lot of the fog from that machine upstairs, and as I said that thing about the fog
machine, he laughed, and said yes, that fog machine can
get to you sometimes, and he leaned over closer to me,
like he was going to tell me some important, secret things,
so I looked at him like I was interested and listening,
meanwhile trying not to smell his whiskeybreath and trying to think of some way to get back to my room.

He started to talk about how he was the manager of
the band, and had been grooming them for a couple of
years now, so they could make a lot of dough, and how
they had all this equipment, like the strobes, and the fog
machine, and a bubble machine, which they hadn't
brought along tonight, since it was being fixed, and how
the equipment really gave the band that little something
extra that you needed to make it with a band these days,
what with all the competition, you really need to be on
your toes all the time, which is why he had been working
on getting the band just right, like finding a real good
drummer, he had hand-picked the drummer for his exciting riffs, you know how the teenybops love anything that

comes out of a drummer, and so he got a lot of loud solos, and how the guitarist and the pianist were both old night-club veterans from the 50's who had gotten into rock for the music and young pussy you got with groupies and all, and that the idea had really worked out well since they were playing at all the high school gyms for dances and were getting a big name in the area, and how he was work-ing on some sort of state tour and maybe a New England tour for some time next year, and how he got all he wanted to drink at these things, and how this line of work beat carney barking, and how he had left the South a few years ago to come north for big money and gotten into rock for the money and he kept leaning closer and closer to me and I suddenly felt scared and very sad and said excuse me and went back into the building.

The band was in between songs when I came back into the room, and there were only a few people standing around, not saying anything, and only a few people sit-ting down, including Tom, who was passed out in his chair. I saw a guy and some girl giving each other a hard time in one corner of the room, because he kept trying to grab her tits, and she didn't want to do shit like that in public, and I walked in a slow circle once or twice, and then left, feeling real bad.

I ran out the door and down the pathway, so I wouldn't have to say anything to that guy in black again, and walked back to my room fast, and sat down on my bed and put my head between my hands, and just rocked back and forth for a while, letting images of carnival bark-ers and the devil and shattered ideas flow in front of my mind's eye for a while, and then I got out Tom's Pleasure Box and found some phenobarbital and scarfed six or eight and washed them down and took off my clothes and crawled into bed. Before I got to sleep I saw the concert again and again inside my head, and then the dance at Fence Club, and the two kept getting mixed together, and I didn't know how to deal with the emotions I was feeling, and then I remembered Woodstock and I rolled over on my side and cried myself to sleep.

T.S. AT YALE

by
Thomas E.
Seus

T. S. is at Yale and he's got one hell of a problem. You see, he completely screwed up his entire life with the help of those institutions which sociologists call "socializing agencies" (agencies which are supposed to help the adolescent mature into a person with sound judgment). His whole sense of having screwed himself lies in the four initials of the organization with which he affiliated himself (as a result of a tragic decision made as a senior in high school)— ROTC. T.S. will be commissioned a 2nd Lieutenant in June; and while his classmates head for Europe, interesting jobs, or whatever their fancy and the draft dictate, he will head for Fort Benning, Georgia, as a newly commissioned *infantry* officer.

I guess it really hurts to know that it wasn't the draft (his number was 289, by the way) but his own free (if idealistically disoriented) will that put him in such an unenviable situation. Unfortunately, T.S. began to see through the shit at twenty-one—when it was too late. If only at seventeen he had known what he knows now, he would never have signed away his individuality then. The army offered all sorts of promises—they would pay his way through any college he could get into. It sounded great to him. He wanted to go to an Ivy League school; and since his father was not a high-grade corporate executive type, money for tuition was not abundant. But it was not this factor as much as his own consciousness which trapped T.S. He was an All-American boy, and his own consciousness was entangled in that myth. He collected thirteen varsity letters in athletics, captained two of the four high school teams he played on, was an elected officer in several school organizations, did well academically, and seemed to be liked and respected by both his teachers and his peers.

He lived in a small community in Westchester County, New York, which was a commuter town of basically high-grade asshole types who made their living in the city. It was the sort of atmosphere that was pervaded by conservatism and patriotism. T.S. fell right under the spell of the mystique that his environment hoped to perpetuate. He felt that serving one's country in the military was an obligation that had to be fulfilled on the way to becoming a high-grade asshole. And he thought it was certainly better to be an officer than an enlisted man. And to get one's way paid through Yale—why, what could be better? T.S. was a modern-day American Adam, an innocent; but he was also an "uptight person in the making"—rigid and goal-oriented. T.S. was easy prey for the Army. He pursued *them,* in fact. The Army symbolized not only money for a Yale education, but also patriotic duty and a firm test of one's masculinity—a continuation of the tests provided by the basketball court or the cross-country course. In all his naiveté, T.S. plunged forward.

Fort Dix, New Jersey, March, 1966. After having wandered around for about eight hours in his jockey shorts, through the various stations of the Army physical examination, T.S. was herded into a room with about sixty other guys, and all were lined up against the four walls with their faces towards the walls. A command was given; everyone in the room dropped his drawers, bent over, and spread his cheeks. A doctor whisked around the room shining a flashlight up everyone's asshole. What the doctor was looking for, T.S. has never figured out. But if T.S. had only understood the symbolism then (everyone in the room was merely a faceless, characterless, potential medium-grade asshole as far as the Army was concerned), he would not have committed himself to an institution more insidious than the insane asylum in Ken Kesey's *One Flew over the Cuckoo's Nest*. T.S. was going to be faced by tough-assed colonels and tyrannical Top Sergeants, instead of by Big Nurse. There was one further piece of symbolism that T.S. was just too naive to comprehend: The Department of the Army sent the form letter notifying him that he was to be a recipient of an Army ROTC scholarship to the person whose name was ahead of his own on the list. He found out about his acceptance by reading about it in a local paper. To the Army he was a nameless body which they were eager to commit to a state of indefinite servitude at the ripe young age of seventeen.

Freshman year at Yale was a bad one for T.S. His consciousness shifted from his combinations of Consciousnesses I and II to a full-fledged Consciousness II; he totally subordinated himself to an organization, the Army. His American dream—that the lone individual can succeed and determine his own fate—was shattered by the reality of Yale. He was not quite as much of a standout, academically, as he thought he would be; and he fell under the sway of a tough Sergeant Major (top enlisted rank in the Army). T.S. became gung-ho; he even joined the rifle team. I guess that the Sergeant Major just scared T.S. with his quaint choice of words. He told T.S. that if he didn't have coitus willingly he just might be castrated (translation: you play ball with us, or you are screwed before you even start your Army career).

T.S. was thoroughly indoctrinated; he accepted the sovereignty of the Army over the individual. Not only was the Army a test of masculinity, but there was also an old Prussian concept of the nobility of military officers which influenced T.S. And would you believe: he actually supported the United States' military position in Vietnam. Those freshman-year bullsessions were really something. Can you imagine T. S. against the rest of Yale (or, at least that's the way it seemed, then—and it would be worse now), arguing about our right to be in Vietnam and how honorable it was to die for such a cause. His heroic philosophy of death came from reading *Man's Fate*. Death, hot damn—the only way to go. T.S. was trapped within the Army mentality—he certainly didn't show any of the brains and rational thinking that the admissions office thought he had when it admitted him to Yale. *I wanna be an airborne ranger, I wanna lead a life of danger, I wanna go to Vietnam, I wanna kill me some Charlie cong.* Imbecile.

Sophomore year, T.S. wasn't quite as gung-ho. He didn't bother to go out for the rifle team. I guess this was partly due to the fact that the Sergeant Major was no longer coach of the team and the threat of having his balls cut off was far less imminent. Also, T.S.'s intelligence was beginning to assert itself a little bit against the confining, conforming Army ethic; that is to say, that instead of spit-shining his shoes and polishing his brass every week, he now only did it once a month. Junior year was better still: he only shined them *once*, all year. And he let his hair grow over his ears—a mortal sin. But there was also a marked change in his perception of the military's position in the world. T.S. felt that we shouldn't be in Vietnam, but that we should get out honorably; of course, only people who live in a world of illusions, as T.S. then continued to do, could ever conceive of this possibility. This was a change, but T.S. still felt that military service was a good character-building experience and prescribed it for one of his screwed-up roommates who was decidedly anti-military. T.S. was, nonetheless, at a point of crisis. And then it happened. . . .

Indiantown Gap Military Reservation, Friday, June 13, 1969. T.S. was driving along Route 22 nearing his destination. He was in Pennsylvania Dutch country, the only place he had ever seen gas stations with rest rooms with vending machines which dispensed six different qualities of condoms. Nice place. T.S. was a little bit early—his orders stated that he didn't have to report until between 0700 and 1300 hours on Saturday (that means between 7:00 A.M. and 1:00 P.M.). He wanted to get there early so that he could relax during the following day. Sheer stupidity. He accidentally drove past the last motel before IGMR and right into the post itself. The sergeant in charge generously offered to let T. S. stay there for the night in one of the barracks and save the money he would have spent on a motel room. T.S. accepted and was immediately put to work, typing for the sergeant. That night, as T.S. tried to get to sleep, he heard the sergeant and another enlisted man discussing the quantity and quality of the various girls that they had laid in recent weeks. It was hard for T.S. to decide which counted for more with this sergeant—the number of girls he had screwed or the number of ribbons that he had as a result of commendations for action on the battlefield. American masculinity—or, why are we *still* in Vietnam. Land of the free, home of the brave, where you can get six different kinds of condoms. Fight on.

Next morning, T.S. was among the first group to be processed in. First of all, they were directed to a parking lot where they were to leave their cars for the next six weeks. They were lined up facing the wall of an old barn-

type building, at attention, no talking, until enough bodies
had accumulated to fill a cattle car (the term of endear-
ment for the large Army transportation trucks) for the trip
to the next station for in-processing. As he stood there, T.S.
kept expecting that at any moment a command would be
given for everyone to strip down and a doctor would come
around examining everyone's dick to make sure that all
met the Army's masculinity standards. Or the traditional
flashlight up the asshole inspection to check the standards
of all these potential medium-grade assholes who were also
potential second lieutenants.

Degradation was the way of life at IGMR; and, as a
result, T.S.'s ambition was to take a piss on the lovely stone
monument that stood at the Reservation's entrance. They
were taught how the enlisted man was treated—by experience. Mess hall was a zoo. Everyone was marched in, some
shit was slopped on each dirty tray, and each animal (excuse me, trainee) shoveled in the shit without lifting his
head. Man, that's really living. T.S.'s messhall rated as the
very worst. When he had K.P., he worked from 0200 until
2130 hours—nineteen and a half hours of pure degradation from the slobs—cooks, that is. One eighteen-year-old
private first class called twenty-one-year-old T.S. "young
man" all day long. By the end of the day, T.S. was about
ready to cram the kid's head into the soapy, greasy water
he had been washing pots in. On the rifle range a runt of
a sergeant said to T.S., "Get your in-tell-igint ass over
here." T.S. complied because he had been stripped of all
genuine traits of manhood the moment he entered into
Army training. He now knew how the draftee felt. *I wanna
be an airborne ranger, I wanna lead a life of danger . . .
everywhere we go, people want to know, who we are, so
we tell them, we are Echo, mighty, might Echo . . . Oh,*

why couldn't he just wake up and find out he was dreaming—but he wasn't.

T.S. saw no reason why they had to waste four or five hours of each day standing in useless formations, why they had to roll their socks and underwear a certain way, why they had to buff the floor every night for an inspection by the pompous little officer who was their platoon evaluator. Discipline is the opiate of mental invalids. T.S. lost some of his faith in humanity when he saw how the gung-ho idiots from certain universities tried to screw you every chance they got—by making you look bad they made themselves look good. With assholes like these filling the ranks of the officer corps, the military is certainly safe from moral improvement for years to come.

November, 1969. Randolph Bourne enters the life of T.S. Bourne's essay, "Below the Battle,"* makes a lot of sense:

> He is one of those young men who, because his parents happened to mate during a certain ten years of the world's history, has had to put his name on a wheel of fate, thereby submitting himself to be drawn into a brief sharp course of military training before being shipped across the sea to kill Germans or be killed by them. He does not like this fate that menaces him, and he dislikes it because he seems to find nothing in the programme marked out for him which touches remotely his aspirations, his impulses, or even his desires . . . He visualizes the obscenity of the battlefield and turns away in nausea. He thinks of the weary regimentation of young men, and is filled with disgust. His mind has turned sour on war and all that it involves. He is poor material for the military proclamation and the drill-sergeant. . . . He

---

* *War and the Intellectuals* (New York: Harper and Row, Publishers, 1964).

feels neither patriotism nor fear, only an apathy toward
the war faintly warmed into a smouldering resentment
at the men who have clamped down the war-pattern upon
him and that vague mass of people and ideas and work-
aday living around him that he thinks of as his country.
. . . War simply did not mix with anything that he had
learned to feel was desirable.

Randolph Bourne, you are T.S.'s prophet. You said it about
World War I, and he feels it about Vietnam. America is
destroying the idealism of its youth. "The Lost Generation
of 1914" in Britain was nothing compared to what you are
in danger of losing, My Beloved Country.

But I have faith that the revolution will come—in a
far different way than anyone has ever thought. There are
two ways that one can fight against the system. One can
wage an external fight, deploring what is going on, but not
really doing anything effective against it. The second way
is to wage an internal fight by getting involved in the machine and stopping it from within. Herbert Marcuse said
that the revolution will come one day when everyone refuses to get out of bed; as a consequence the whole system
is brought to a complete standstill. The revolution just
might come about in a stranger way.

T.S. accepts the idealism expressed by Randolph
Bourne, and his own changed consciousness allows him to
see through the shit these days. T.S. will be one of a new
breed of Army officer—one who values humanity over
discipline, peace over war, life over death. There will be
others like him, and they will bring the machine to a halt
from within. A few months back, the news media carried
a story about an infantry company that refused an order
to move out. Someday that incident will be repeated on a
greater scale with an impact that will rock the world.

The revolution will happen this way: the colonel will issue an order to move out and capture a certain strategic area, and he will be answered by young voices on his radio —"Sir, Alfa Company is NOT moving out . . . Sir, Bravo Company is NOT moving out . . . Sir, Charlie Company is NOT moving out . . . Sir, Delta Company is NOT moving out." And over in 1st Battalion, the situation will be the same. In the adjacent units, the young officers will be repeating the same act of insubordination and willful disobedience—they will have stopped the machine by affirming their idealism, their revolutionary consciousness, and their humanitarian spirit. Have faith, my friends, in T.S. and others like him.

THE
SUMMER
AT FRANKLIN ARMS

by
Jonathan
Sternberg

Franklin Arms would be something else again. My grandmother had suggested that I could probably get the job for the summer, and I figured that being a lifeguard wouldn't be all that bad, even if all of the residents were over sixty. I would be outdoors all summer, and there would be lots of income with few expenses, and I wouldn't have to commute on the lunatic Long Island Railroad every day to New York. I knew ahead of time what the disadvantages of the job might include. There would be no lovely girls lolling around the pool, and with the exception of my unknown partner (whose grandmother had set him up too) there wouldn't be any college kids around. There was only one day off per week, which meant that I wouldn't have much time to see my other friends, since I had to work both Saturdays and Sundays. Visitors were out of the question for me. I also knew that the particular idiosyncrasies of two hundred aging Jewish grandmothers (and grandfathers) could probably drive the unwary teenager to the wall or even further. I had been forewarned by the newspaper delivery boy, whom I happened to meet one day before accepting the job. I saw him arguing with a woman who was holding a rolled newspaper as though she intended to use it on him. After she stormed away, I asked him what it had been all about.

"I can't stand this place anymore," he fumed. "I'm quitting. These goddamn people drive me crazy."

"What was she so excited about?" I asked.

"That woman is such an idiot," he said. "She wants me to wrap her paper in some kind of brown bag, and tie it up with string. She thinks I'm some kind of gift-wrapping service. Or maybe she thinks it rains in her corridor and she wants me to keep the paper safe and dry. It's the same thing with half the people in this building."

"Why, do they all ask you to wrap their papers up like that?"

"No, each one has something special. One guy said to put it under the mat a special way. The next guy tells you to put it under a different way. Some tell you not to put it under the mat at all, they want it on the mat, or they want it folded in half or in thirds, or tucked under or out. It's incredible. One old deaf man wants me to stand there and ring on the bell every day so I can deliver the paper to him in person. I rang for ten minutes before he heard me, and that was enough of that."

"They aren't all like that, are they?"

"No, there are some nice people here, but on the whole they drive you crazy." Having finished his brief explanation, he picked up his canvas bag and headed out the door.

On my first day at the job, I decided to arrive fifteen minutes early; I figured that there would be a lot to do, and I would get off to a good start. When I arrived, I walked through the lobby, down a corridor, past two glass doors, up some winding stairs, and out to the pool deck. It was empty. The only sound I heard was the sound of waves breaking on the beach one hundred yards away. I looked around. The sun deck was one expanse of gray tile, broken only by the placid blue waters of the pool. There were several small pavilions for shade. Around the outer edges of the patio there were bridge chairs, and chaise lounges without cushions, each marked with the owner's name. I looked down the row. Solomon. Reizman, Rifkin, Selzer, Greenwald, Grossman, Levy, Lifshitz, and Stein, ad infinitum. No doubt about who lived here. I looked up at the seven-story building which surrounded the deck on three sides. Each apartment had a little terrace, which jutted out like a cliff, and each terrace was enclosed, so you couldn't see what was going on. They all looked exactly alike, except for one or two flower pots which occasionally graced a ledge. At the ground level, around the perimeter of the building, there were raised beds of shrubs and flowers, like the kind they have at Jones Beach, except that these were meticulously trimmed and nurtured. I was back in the Garden of Eden, and there was the oversized Fountain of Youth, right in the middle. I don't know how long I stood there day-dreaming; finally I went back inside to find out what was supposed to be going on. As I came into the lobby, I saw another kid standing next to two older men. One older man approached me.

"Good morning, Steve, you're right on time."

"Are you Mr. Zimmerman?" He nodded. "My name is Jonathan."

"Oh oh oh," he apologized, "I'm sorry. I had you mixed up with my nephew, Steve." He smiled and introduced me to Phil, who was working with me. Then he introduced me to Jim, the superintendent, who was going to show us around the pump room and explain the job of maintaining the pool. "Boys," Mr. Zimmerman said, with a kindly half grin, "I want you to listen to everything Jim tells you. If you have any problems with the pool itself, I want you to tell him, and we'll get them straightened out. That's the first thing." We went downstairs to check out the pump room, and learned all about the chlorine pump, the filters and the backwash. Then we went upstairs to look at the vacuum cleaner. All along the way, Mr. Zimmerman was explaining the nature of our job.

"You'll want to get here by nine each morning, so you can attend to the pool and clean up the deck before anyone comes down. When the people come down, you get them their chaise cushions, or their card tables or whatever they want, and set everything up for them. We'll see that everyone in the house takes care of you boys each week, because I know you're going to do a fine job, and we think you should be paid for it." The mention of money brought a twinkle to his eyes. Mr. Zimmerman had made a fortune in fertilizer, the last place anyone ever looked for a fortune.

We came back to the pool deck, which was as empty as before. Mr. Zimmerman mentioned that most of the people never came down before lunch, but they liked to watch from their windows and see the pool boys cleaning up the deck. "When you finish cleaning the deck, I want you boys to stay on your feet, and look busy. One thing the people here dislike is laziness." He said it not to chastise us, but rather as a matter of policy. "On the other hand, you don't have to do every last thing they ask of you. Some of these people would have you run upstairs for their slippers for them, and we want you to stay down here all the time at the pool. That's your first responsibility."

He showed us how to use the vacuum cleaner, which didn't work too well. What was worse was the fact that the neighboring building incinerated its garbage every day at noon, and the ashes inevitably settled in our pool. That was a problem, because Mr. Zimmerman insisted that we vacuum early in the morning, even though the worst came down at noon. While we were vacuuming, some people came out to the sun deck. They all came over to introduce themselves, and a few stood around watching us operate the clumsy vacuum cleaner. "Why don't you hold it *this* way," somebody asked, twisting his wrists to demonstrate. "You could work faster that way." A brief argument ensued, after which Phil agreed to try several variations to placate everyone concerned. That was the beginning of lesson number one at Franklin Arms. Everyone wants to call the shots, be the boss.

To fulfill this urge, the board of directors had conceived a plan which put almost everyone into some position of authority. (Bureaucracy? Franklin Arms doesn't know from bureaucracy! We've got something better!) Mr. Zimmerman was the Pool Director. There was Jimmy Alexander, the Social Committee Chairman, who told us to come to him if there were any problems. There was Hy Milton, the Pool Deck Chairman, who looked like Santa Claus, who urged us to speak to *him* if there were any problems. I began to feel that most of these people just wanted someone, anyone, to talk to them. In addition, there were Joe Rothman, Jake Altman, and Jerry Dietz, who were all on the House Committee; they said we should speak to them too, about any problems. Most of these people created more problems for us than anything else, because two or more of them would inevitably argue over everything we did. Sometimes they argued among themselves, and sometimes they argued with the other residents; it was their *modus vivendi.*

"Everyone thinks he is the boss," Mr. Schlover used to say. He was in fact the boss, President of Franklin Arms. Mr. Schlover looked like a Don Martin cartoon character drawn in a fit of comic anger. He had a huge belly, which hung over tiny hips and slender legs that were never once revealed, even during the worst heat of the summer. His face was covered by a dour little moustache which seemed to bend his lips into a perpetual scowl. He used to rest his two hands in the natural crevice formed where his belly joined his chest, in a way that suggested that J. P. Morgan was not really gone after all. That's who he reminded me of. "Yes, they think they are all bosses," he said. He was referring to a group of women who had just come out to the pool deck. A moment ago they had been standing in the lobby with Mr. Schlover, watching the droplets of water drip from the ceiling to the floor.

"It looks like the pipes are leaking," Mrs. Lowenstein had said.

"No, it's only sweating a little. The pipes always sweat during the summer months. It's a healthy sign."

"I'm telling you, Sol, I think it's a leak, and you should call a plumber before we're all flooded out of here!" Most of the women had agreed with Mrs. Lowenstein, and while Mr. Schlover called himself a democrat, he was really incensed that anyone should question his authority. "Who told you what was wrong here? Since when are you supposed to be a plumber?" These last words were undoubtedly followed by a tiny smile which meant that the argument was over, and let's all go outside to the pool. Within a few hours plumbers were called in to examine the pipes, and after ripping the ceiling apart they discovered a serious leak which took two days to repair.

By eleven o'clock, Phil and I had finished everything we could think of doing. More people began to arrive, and they requested our help. Most of the men wanted bridge tables and chairs set up so they could pursue their endless card games. It was interesting to watch them play, although you didn't do that too long, because you would be accused of sluffing off. The women, on the other hand, wanted you to set up their chaise lounges and their umbrellas, so they could sit around the pool, reading, or, in most cases, simply chatting. The women were very clique conscious: there were unmarked but very real boundaries between the groups of chaises that made up each group.

Even within these groups there was a distinct pecking order. People were very fussy about that; you didn't move any chaise lounge without the owner's permission, nor did you lend anyone an umbrella or chaise which didn't belong to her. Sometimes there were complications, as with Mrs. Bauer and Mrs. Burke, who shared one umbrella together. When I brought it out for them, an argument developed over where to place the umbrella so that both could be shaded. The debate caught me totally unprepared, as I stood moving the umbrella from one side to the other. Finally one told the other to stop shouting like a peddler's wife, and then stormed off in a rage.

Most of the people were less demanding, and the first afternoon passed by without further incident. Phil and I got along really well. At about four-thirty we started to collect the chaise lounge cushions from benches whose owners had gone upstairs; by five-thirty everyone was gone, and we were finishing stacking the cushions under a canvas cover. We were about to jog along the beach and take a swim in the ocean. "You know," Phil remarked, "I noticed something really funny about these people."

"Only one thing?" I asked. We both laughed.

"No, really. Don't you think it's kind of funny that we're called lifeguards?"

"You mean because we're more like cabana boys, with the chairs and everything?"

"Yeah, but not just that. We spent all morning cleaning up that pool, but no one went in the water all day. It just sat there, totally empty!"

A few people had stuck their feet into the water, and some of the women had sat on the steps at the shallow end of the pool. But no one had actually plunged in.

.   .   .

After the first few days, Phil and I settled into the routine. We would arrive around nine and finish cleaning up by ten. During the next two hours we would just sit and talk, waiting for someone to come down to the pool. We talked about the people who lived there.

"Have you heard about this Mrs. Fess?" Phil asked.

"No, who is she?"

"I haven't seen her yet, but one of the men was telling me to watch out for her. They say she's really nuts." There was a pause. "Mr. Alexander said that she goes up to the card room every night and plays poker with the men. She always loses, but she keeps playing anyway. They say she rattles on and on about how she used to be such a great cardplayer in her youth, which must have been a hundred years ago. It drives all of the men nuts."

"Why don't they just tell her that they don't want to play with her?"

"They said she's really old, and kind of eccentric, and she wouldn't understand. Besides, she's just donated three walnut card tables to the card room, and everyone likes to use them. So they can't really kick her out."

"What are they going to do about her?" I asked.

"Wait until she kicks the bucket, I guess." It wasn't a very funny comment, nor was it meant to be. People were always dying at Franklin Arms. The strange thing about it was the irreverent attitude displayed by the other members of the house. "Remember this one," they used to say, "he's been pushin' daisies for two years already! Pushin' daisies, all right."

Our conversation was cut short by the arrival of one of our many bosses. He had a job for us. It was amazing, some of the things they devised to keep us busy. This morning they wanted us to scrub the ring of tiles which lined

the top of the pool. To get to the tiles, you had to crawl
along the edge of the pool and lean over the side, and
reach under water with a brush. It was going to be a full
day's work. While I was scrubbing, a small group of people gathered around me. Eventually someone asked me
what kind of soap I was using. I knew it was a loaded
question.

Me: "I think it's Joy."

Mrs. Siegel: "Joy? That's no good. Who told you to
use Joy?"

Me: "Mr. Zimmerman gave it to me."

Mrs. Siegel: "Max Zimmerman! What does he know
about soap? You wait right here, I'll bring you a little Ajax
from my house. That's the only way to get it clean."

Mrs. Gerber: "And what's wrong with Joy? I use it
in my house all the time on everything."

Mrs. Siegel: "But your house isn't a pool. He needs
something to clean a pool, not a house!"

Irrefutable logic. It didn't really matter what kind of
soap I was using; I could have been using anything else,
and there still would have been a debate about it, because
that's the way these people lived. In the back of their minds
they were all concerned for the appearance of the pool; in
the front of their minds they wanted to make sure that
everyone else knew how very concerned they were. "Joy,"
Mrs. Siegel was muttering as she walked away, "what does
Max Zimmerman know about Joy?" A good question, I
thought. He doesn't even know how to smile.

Actually, he did smile from time to time. Every time
he called me Steve, he smiled. He also smiled the day he
bribed the county pool inspector not to close the pool because our chlorine pump was temporarily out of order. He
was funny about the chlorine level, which had to be tested

every few hours by dropping some chemicals into a test tube sample of pool water and comparing the resulting colors to a colored plastic calibrated scale. "Now boys," he said, "when you check to see the color of the sample, you have to hold it up to the sunlight to get the true color." If the colors didn't match properly, he would then hold the sample over the pool, or sometimes over the gray tiles, until the sample matched the scale. Then he would say, "You see, boys, you have to hold it over the tiles. If you hold it up to the sun, it appears too light!" In point of fact, he changed his method every day, depending on whether the chlorine sample was too dark, or too light. On any given day the procedure that produced the desired results was hailed as the proper way to make the test.

During the course of the summer it became clear that the only people who were going to use the pool besides me and Phil were a few grandchildren who came to visit. One of these was Melanie, Mr. Schlover's ten-year-old grand-daughter. We got along pretty well, although I think I was envious of the freedom she had to argue with her grandfather. Mr. Schlover would come down to the pool and say, "Melanie, it's time to come out of the pool. Your grandmother wants you to come up and eat lunch."

"Tell her I'll be up in a minute, Gramps."

"No, Melanie, I want you to come up now, you've had enough swimming for one morning. Come up and have lunch!" In response, Melanie would usually swim over to the side of the pool, take a mouthful of water and squirt it in the direction of her grandfather. He would scowl, and then tell me to order Melanie out of the pool, as though my position as lifeguard represented some final, undeniable authority. At first I resented this tactic, but later I began to feel that it didn't really matter, since she had already made her point and could then leave the pool graciously at my behest.

Some of the other children were not so lucky. It seemed like someone was always yelling for one of the kids to stay in shallow water, stop playing games in the pool, or come out of the water altogether. There was one eight-year-old girl, Cindy, who swam better than I did. She was always the subject of Mr. Schlover's lecture on why children should not be allowed to play in the deeper end of the pool. "It's dangerous, you know, very dangerous. We're not covered; what if something should happen to her, and we're not covered?" I used to wonder, what if something should happen to her and we *were* covered?

Whenever Mr. Schlover approached Cindy in the pool she would swim away. She used to tell me, "I don't like Mr. Schlover; he's always trying to boss me around." I used to empathize with her, since that was my problem too.

By the end of the summer, Phil and I were more than ready to quit. We discovered that we held the peculiar distinction of being the first pair of lifeguards to ever complete a summer at Franklin Arms. It was understandable why so many guys before us had quit or been fired. The people there demanded a million things—everything except that we watch the pool, because no one ever did go in.

That was incredible to me. They paid a fortune for the pool, kept it in perfect shape, and hired two kids to attend to the pool every summer. It was as though the pool was supposed to be some kind of untouchable monument, maybe something forbidden. Towards the end of the summer an incident occurred which seemed to bear this out. I had been offering swimming lessons to the kids. One morning Mr. Lutz came to speak to me about swim-

ming lessons; he wanted to learn to swim. I told him anyone could learn, and promised to start lessons the next day.

I thought it would be great to see him actually using
the pool during the week; perhaps if he started, others
would follow. He was a corpulent man; I was sure that he
could float and gradually learn to swim. It turned out that
I was totally wrong. We had two lessons, during which I
tried every approach I could think of. Kickboards, lifejack-
ets and floats were no help. The side stroke was out. Nothing worked. At the end of the second lesson, he was ready
to quit. I went out to lunch, wondering how I could encourage him to try again. As I came back to the pool deck, I
saw a large crowd of women standing around the edge of
the pool, shouting and waving hysterically. I ran to the
pool; Phil was standing there, soaking wet and out of
breath. Someone was huddled under a pile of towels.

"Phil, what happened! Was anyone hurt?"

"I don't know. I don't remember what happened. I
just jumped in and pulled him out."

The women were still yelling, each trying to be heard
above the rest. I turned around. Mr. Lutz was sitting
quietly in the midst of the uproar. I asked him if he was
O.K., and he nodded. When I asked him what happened,
he smiled. "When you were gone, I decided to go back to
the pool and try to swim again. I was thinking maybe if
I tried to lie down on my back I could float. I tried it but
I couldn't stay up." In fact he had gone right to the bottom,
flat on his back in less than three feet of water.

I left Franklin Arms that summer figuring I would
never see the place again. The next summer I went back.

ALEXANDER

by
Ralph
Halsey

Many people change consciousness while at a university, and the forms of their changes and the lasting effects on each individual's life vary greatly. One could discount this change as an empirical part of the process that college students always undergo, but I think that this is a simplistic approach to the situation. Environmental changes are bound to effect some changes in any individual, and the environment of a college campus is vastly different than that from which most students come. In my sophomore year, as a requirement for a psychology course, I did a personality study of another member of the class. In my case this was a close friend. The study was done over two months and consisted of many tests and interviews. As is pointed out in my paper, Alexander (as my subject was known) had changed a great deal from freshman year to the spring of sophomore year, when the paper was written. The further change in his consciousness, from the boy described in the paper to the person I know today, is truly astounding and a sign that in fact there is hope for the cultural and social revolution that many envision for the United States.

In the spring of his sophomore year, Alexander's consciousness could at best be described as minimal and at worst as nonexistent. Not only did he lack concern for what went on within his own mind (and the minds of others), he lacked knowledge of the existence of most of his inner feelings. He plodded through his junior year by playing hockey and surrounding himself with a group of friends, none of whom he really had any strong commitment to.

Through his bursary job in the admissions office, he was given a seat on the powerful Dwyer Commission, concerned with alumni affairs. On this commission he was surrounded by a group of very powerful and influential members of the corporate establishment. As a part of his duties on the commission he gave speeches to alumni groups around the country, most of the time offering only nebulous pleas for understanding and help and a call for faith in President Brewster. By Alexander's own admission, they involved little thought on his part; he repeated over and over what he thought the alumni wanted to hear.

During the spring vacation the Dwyer Commission traveled to the West Coast, which Alexander had seen very little of. His reflections on this trip are interesting, for he was impressed not by the differences between himself and the youth of California, Oregon and Washington, but by the similarities between the alumni there and the alumni he knew all over the rest of the country. During this vacation Alexander accepted a summer job in New York with the firm of one of the commission's members.

Alexander returned to New Haven to find the campus highly politicized. For the first time he saw that many people around him were very concerned about the state of the country. He was very cynical about the events that preceded the strike in late April and early May and took no part in them. He attended many of the rallies, but solely for their entertainment value. By the time of the May First demonstration, Alexander had become aware of many things that he had not known to have existed in any way. He had never before noticed the presence and power of revolutionary groups. He was for the first time confronted with a great number of people who preached an ideology entirely the opposite from that on which he had been raised. He was taken from the bigotry of his parents and the people he grew up with into a total focus on the

Black Panthers and what they stood for. Alexander was
politicized. Never before had he thought so much about
his place in society and society's relationship to groups like
the Panthers. Alexander was very moved.

He was the organizer of a petition signed by more
than three thousand students that called for an alumni
vote of confidence for Brewster's defense of the Panthers.
Although he was by no means a member of the campus
revolutionary vanguard, his opinions and considerations
had changed. It was a gradual process, and even Alexander himself did not realize the change that was taking
place within himself. His first realization came in the middle of May, when he was asked by the Dwyer Commission
to talk to a group of alumni who were concerned about
the recent events at Yale. I have heard several accounts of
what occurred that night in Chicago, and they all concur
with Alexander's story. The meeting was held in a large
hall. About one hundred and fifty of the wealthiest Chicago alumni attended. The topic under discussion was the
May First demonstration in New Haven, and what it indicated for the future of Yale. Many local men gave their
views on the situation, and although none of them had
been in New Haven that weekend, they all seemed to be
experts on the situation. Their presentation of the events
of the weekend was made solely from what they had read
or heard through the mass media or from friends in New
Haven. According to Alexander, few of their stories were
close to the truth, and it was obvious that no attempt at
factual accuracy was being made. After an hour or two
of outrageous slandering of anyone in any way connected
with May First, one alumnus asked Alexander to comment on the situation in New Haven that weekend. At this
point Alexander was about to explode, and he realized that

something had to be done to salve his conscience about this meeting. He stepped to the microphone and uttered a very short, but wholly effective sentence. He said to the wealthiest and most conservative group of men in Chicago, "Jerry Rubin was right, you are nothing but a bunch of fucking assholes." Alexander's consciousness had reached a new level. As he stormed from the hushed room, he began for the first time to think of this group with absolute abhorrence.

Needless to say, the Chicago alumni demanded an explanation, and although Alexander is not sure, he thinks that Brewster probably quieted the situation down.

With great reservation, Alexander began his job in New York. He disliked the work from the beginning and the people he met confirmed his recent discovery of the evils of the corporate state. He continued at his job with feelings of increasing revulsion for the people who employed him. After a month he resigned and headed for the home of a friend in California.

He was unable to convince his parents that he could no longer work in New York. Their pressure for him to return to New York became unbearable, and a mutually accepted schism developed between parents and child.

In California Alexander looked up his brother, who at this time was a wealthy junior executive in a large California firm. His brother gave Alexander the same arguments about going back to New York that he had heard from his parents, and Alexander dismissed his brother as being yet another member of the large, but inexcusable, corporate state. Alexander spent about a month traveling around the West, staying with friends and meeting the younger people that he had missed on his first visit to that area. His life-style changed considerably. Besides the obvious physical changes that took place, Alexander for the first time in his life found that he could enjoy a great deal more than just hockey. It was a complete renaissance. Had he met up with a group like the Kesey crowd, Alexander might never have left it. As it was, he came back to the East Coast only after many days of deliberation weighing the advantages of staying against the expediency of going back to finish school. He decided upon the latter and returned to Yale without any word from his parents in Boston.

My first conversation with Alexander in September continued over about three weeks during countless meals and meetings on the streets. It was very difficult for me to comprehend his complete change. For the first time since I had known him, Alexander talked of people and the places those people lived in. He spoke of the many loves and friendships he had developed over the summer in California. He spoke of the life-style he had now come to love so much. He told of the land he had discovered, of trees and mountains and rivers and lakes that he had never seen as being anything but pragmatic fixtures for everyday life. He related stories of Mexicans he had seen while on the Coast, and how he had been unable to convince his brother that something should be done by his brother's company to change the employment situation in California and the whole country.

His feeling of helplessness was increased by the fact that many of the people he knew at Yale were unable to accept him on his new terms. His frustrations were evident, but for the first time they were not manifested in aggressive behavior. Alexander had lost the chip on his shoulder and was able to get along even with people who were vehemently denouncing him. He continued with his hockey, but even in his approach to that he developed very new attitudes. He began to enjoy the sport itself, something he had never done before. He began to draw, and he pursued other creative pastimes that he once had called the stupid amusements of fools. Alexander found a girl, and his transformation from the aggressive, narrow-minded young man he had been to the highly conscientious and considerate person that he is today was complete. At the age of twenty-one he has, in fact, begun to live, and he is overwhelmed by the experience.

Alexander's experience is in no way unique. One can see countless students here and at other universities experiencing the same awakening process, but the test of real cultural change lies in the depth and strength of each individual's commitment. Many of those people who have adopted a new life-style in college will revert to the life of their parents within months after they leave the college community. They will call this reversion "growing up" and will persecute those whom they feel have not "grown up." Alexander's brother has told me that Alexander's development is "just a phase of life" and that Alexander will surely grow out of it and then be able to settle down.

Alexander's brother is wrong, and will be proved wrong in a very short time when Alexander forsakes business and law schools and a job with his family company to search through this country and Europe for new people and places rather than settling into the stagnant life of the corporate state that he has come to dislike. He is beyond the stage where wealth and monetary security mean anything to him. He wants instead the peace found on Big Sur in the solitude of a camp by the sea or in a winter retreat in mountains free of snowmobiles and skiers.

PART

III

A LETTER TO HOME

by
Peter
Mareneck

Dear Mom and Dad:

I am writing to you hoping that I can explain something about the way I'm living now, why I have chosen this way, and where I think it will lead me in the future. I've gone through a lot of changes since I left home a year and a half ago, and if I had to characterize it all in one image, I'd say I've stopped worrying about what I'm going to "do for society" and turned myself toward living a full and happy life with a small community of people. You see, I've found that to be happy you don't need to be "successful," you don't need to be an expert, you don't need to be stable and rational and predictable. You don't even need to read how to do it in books. All you need is a crazy, naïve ideal and lots of hard-workin' energy—energy that comes out of the heart, out of the imagination, out of the thin air.

You see, for as long as I can remember I've always thought and been taught that before I could begin to do anything really significant for others I would have to go through all the long and grueling stages of training and accomplishment that it takes to become a "successful" man, a man with enough power to really do some good for the world. My whole psychological pattern of dealing with the world was built upon the modern scientific method: collect all the data, draw up the theory, practice a lot in the "lab," and then go out and save the world. And so I aimed everything for my "golden future." I regarded the family as a practice pad for school; high school as the testing lab for college; college as the proving ground for grad school; and grad school the key to getting a groovy, socially potent job in which I could finally put all my preparation to work and begin to make my dreams come true.

And so it was that I left you all at home and trundled

off to college, the valiant young knight who had things all figured out and assured, as long as he kept to the schedule. Yet down deep I was empty. The only place I really existed was at the theoretical level. When I tried to define just who I was, all I got was what I *thought* about this and that. Nowhere was there a "what I am doing about it." I got nauseated at myself. I felt foolish and weak and stagnant. And completely alone.

However, I continued along in the same old way until last spring, when, after becoming totally disillusioned with our "great social process," I finally realized that if I really wanted to do something meaningful for others, I couldn't expect to do it in a way that treated people like impersonal objects. And I couldn't expect to begin helping *after* I had "made it" for myself; it had to begin right now. And it had to begin with the people who were right around me, people I already had a personal relationship with, my friends. I realized that if I wasn't able to give myself fully to a small tribe of people, I could never expect to give anything to the world at large. Because it's only by living today the way it's supposed to be after the "revolution" that one can effect an immediate and constructive change.

For me it has simply come to this: if you've got a vision of how life can be better, then don't go messin' around trying to push your ideas over from the podium: get it together in your own backyard and then invite the neighbors over for dinner.

But does this mean that drop-out-ism is my answer? Does it mean that we should all just forget about the rest of the world and have a good time with our friends? Not quite. What I'm pointing to is a method of living which I feel is the only viable way left for finding a whole-sum life within this huge, depersonalized, technocratic mess we call modern society. And this method is the development of a new social unit: the communal family, a family something like the one I've been living with here at Skokorat Road.

The reason I believe so strongly in the communal style is that it allows a person to live on a scale that remains personal and yet provides for intense social interaction and support. It allows a group of people to interrelate on a direct, intimate, and honest level. Honesty is probably the most important ingredient in making a commune successful; no matter *what* goes on between the members, it will happen in a way in which everyone feels he can express himself fully—without fear of rejection, jealousy, or evil intent. For the whole point of communal living is to open one's life: to destroy the haunting fears of exposing one's real self to others. The self that includes one's habits, affections, aggressions, and selfishness as well as one's good sides. It means *inviting* the members of your family to respond to and criticize you in depth, rather than trying to hide your inner self from them by becoming an impregnable bastion of individualism.

So many of us have been conditioned to believe that being able to achieve a state of total independence and objectivity toward others is a sign of strength and maturity. Therefore we have been taught that the way to live a safe and successful life is to be able to define ourselves and others in as concise a little bag as possible, so that we can always keep proper perspective and control of the situation.

But to me communal life means not only breaking down this myth that a person must always maintain a safe distance of objectivity between himself and others; it also means one must go beyond devoting his life to just a nuptial partner and their offspring. It means committing one-self to an expanded family of single as well as conjugal members. It has for too long been a crime that people who don't get married and fit themselves into a neat little nuclear family have been ostracized as cold, unloving people. Single individuals can contribute just as much to a family as anyone else, and they should be allowed the enjoyment of participating in the process of raising children, even if they aren't the procreators of those children.

I realize now that love and shared responsibility, the two most fundamental forces in any family, are not one-to-one experiences. I know that I can not restrict myself to loving just one person at a time. I feel I will have to go beyond the age-old form of dedicating myself to my one-and-only spouse and our children. Not because that form is wrong, but because it isn't enough anymore. There are just too many people in the world now. Personal responsibility and care must increase to involve five or ten "spouses"; not in the old sense of the word, but in a new expanded family. In other words, although I may be "based" in one woman or one man, I must be able to take the love, trust, and energy from that relationship and spread it into another, and another, and another. I must be willing to care for and respect each member of my communal family as I would my wife, and as I would my children, even as I would my parents. Which also means that I must resign myself from any hope of being "king of my own castle" in the sense that I too must be spouse, parent, and child to every other member of the household.

This brings up the question of marriage. Because I believe in living communally, I don't put as much value on permanent marriage as I think you do. Not that I would ever deny that the man-woman unit will continue to be the basic human relationship for a long time to come, but I do feel that only if we begin to live in relation to numerous individuals with the same commitment for support, growth, and fulfillment as you have towards one other person, will we begin to move towards transforming society into a cooperative, instead of competitive, collectivity.

I don't mean by this that one should set himself up a harem or involve himself on an equally intensive sexual relationship with all the members of his family. That is something that will continue to remain a matter of personal expression between two individuals. But what I mean by being a spouse is that one should work to develop the emotional intimacy that a man traditionally shows only to his wife. This intimacy extends to single members as well as members who have joined themselves in some kind of personal union beyond being commune brethren. So that although there probably won't be complete freedom and equality of sexual expression among members, there will be freedom of emotional interrelating.

But in order to develop such relationships we will have to be willing to change our situation and start over again if need be. No one can expect to find ten or twenty people who they can love like a spouse at their first try. And no one should be condemned for trying over and over again until he finds such a group. Marriage is a personal relationship that evolves, as the persons involved create a multi-dimensional love between themselves. Love for me is an organic thing; it is subject to growth and decline as the persons loving go through different stages in their lives. Love isn't some category of interrelating you achieve by doing certain things for, or with, another person—it's a *way* of doing things. It's not just assuming the responsibility for another person so that you take care of her when she is sick or give her money when she's broke; but it's sharing feelings, and sharing fears, and exchanging criticism in a kind and helpful way. Real loving means being "out front" with another person: open about everything you are and everything you experience the other to be. Then, no matter what you do with that other person, be it building goat stalls, cooking dinner, or exchanging delicate personal criticism, it will end up being a tension-releasing growth experience that extends one's awareness of his meaning for others rather than increasing his self-consciousness and defensiveness.

To pull off this great ideal of mine is proving to be an incredibly difficult thing, for it means sharing the same physical facilities, the maintenance responsibilities, the child-caring tasks, and most importantly, the decision-making. And yet I wouldn't trade these "hardships" for anything. Because although communal living means a lot of physical and psychological sweat, it also means a lot of freedom. For instance, when you are sharing finances and other group responsibilities, it means that not everyone has to work all the time. Two people don't have to do the same task twice, as they would if they were living apart or in nuclear families. The others will allow each member time off to do whatever he wants to; to be alone, to get himself together. In fact, making sure there is always an opportunity for any member to be alone for introspective meditation, self-expression, or whatever reason, is one of the foremost necessities that we've encountered in our commune. The collective aspect of life is one dimension of the intentional community; equally important is the individual dimension, for it is only after an individual is honest and confident within his own self that he will be able to be honest and giving in the family group.

I've found this year that the horrible pressure of forced and scheduled responsibility has been eliminated by living with people who trust and care about each other enough to make sure that things which need doing get done. Tasks get taken care of not because someone makes us do them, and not because we have to do them to keep up with the folks next door; but because we want to do them, we expect to do them, no matter how "menial" they might be, because we really believe in the welfare of our family. Our communal responsibility is not just altruism, either; it's practical, in that it allows each individual more time to be free to do what he wants.

Another liberating aspect of living communally is that the demand to become specialized and restricted to one permanent role is eliminated. The members of a communal family, by their numbers and commitment to sharing, allow each other the opportunity to change roles, in society as well as in the family; providing the necessary free time to learn new skills and develop new ideas.

Finally, the element of communal living that I feel is of utmost significance is spirituality. For I have found that once you turn away from the social-achievement-competition scene, you naturally move toward spiritual development and expression. One's care for the commune of persons evolves into care for the commune of nature, for the commune of animals, for the commune of the world, and for the commune of God. To share God with a brother is the highest form of worship that I know, and by that sharing, the divine magic is strengthened and made experienceable. The "communal spirit" is part of that wonderful magic that each of us is invested with: the power to create, to transform something lonely and lifeless and afraid into something alive and growing and happy.

Finally I would like to say a few words about the pro-
verbial topics of difference between parents and children
of this generation: drugs, sex, and politics. I feel the older
generation makes all of these issues into much bigger deals
than I deem them worthy of. To me, politics is only valuable and relevant when it exists as a constructive dialogue
between two individuals, aimed at creating a new and better relationship between them. Anything more than this
only leads to misunderstanding and alienation. Sex is only
needed and valuable when it exists as an emotional dialogue between two people, aimed at creating a deeper relationship between them. Anything more than this only
leads to selfishness and pain. And drug use is only valuable
and constructive when it exists as an exploratory dialogue
between an individual and his hidden inner being. Anything more than this only leads to escapism and enslave-
ment. All three can be amazingly useful and creative and
something to be enjoyed by everyone, but only so long as
they are respected forms of *personal* expression; beyond
that arena of one-to-one experience, they only lead to re-
ification and dehumanization.

So in conclusion, I sure can't say that I've made it to
the ultimate state; not by any means. I still live with sor-
row and depressions and disappointments. I certainly
haven't succeeded in any great social engineering or improvement projects, and I haven't even improved the status of one indigent citizen. But I have created a foundation
on which I can build and share my energy and hope with
other people in this world. And I feel that if each one of
us could share the kind of experience that I share with my
new family, then maybe we wouldn't need any great social
engineering projects to raise the status of the world. All
I can say is that I really feel happy with my life and con-

fident that by living communally I can best share that happiness with others. Again, this message is only me at this point in my journey. Which is to say that things could change any time. But no matter how I am living, I hope that we can keep close together; at least in understanding if not in belief, in love if not in life-style.

Enough words for now,
Peter

HELLO...

Charles H.
    Levin

Words do not mean much. Somewhere in these words there is a face, my face. Perhaps you will see it, or feel it; but you must believe that I am looking at you. I have no answers to give you. You know all that there is to know; only you and I do not always see what we know. Man, you and I hide among our fears and lash out with lances of ignorance—war. I once turned the music of a stereo down to a very slow speed. An echo-chamber device magnified the sounds of music. They became the sounds of a distant battlefield. I heard the explosions and the horrifying reverberations of shells piercing the earth. There was death in the music. There was war. The following words are a possibility:

> Announcement to the populace: By order of the Supreme Power all music is banned. This is a measure that will ensure peace. Studies have shown that sublimation of musical tones causes increased violence in *Homo Sapiens* . . . All those who do not cease and desist from the composition of, production of, and listening to music will be decomposed upon discovery.

I love music. I want to listen to the melodies of men as long as I am able. "Able" is a word with varied implications; he was also brother to Cain.

I attended a party not so long ago, a celebration of the birth of Jesus of Nazareth, the Christ. The people who were giving the affair were Jewish by heritage. The house was decorated in lavish fashion: an ornate evergreen tree, red sashes fringing the fireplace, holly suspended from the door jambs and window sills. The guests were show business notables, people you and I have seen and heard

on the media's air and sound waves. These guests all huddled together in the smallest rooms of a large house, talking, drinking constantly, listening, walking, sweating,
filling their bladders. I could not talk; I could only sweat.
I smiled as they shook my hand and walked past me. I
was not an oasis. They did not stop to drink of my waters
or shade themselves in my eyes. They seemed to pass by
like apparitions into the crowd where one could be alone.
My head throbbed. The noise was deafening. I needed to
be held. I left, very ill.

HelloHelloHelloHelloHelloHelloHelloHelloHelloHelloHello

There were fourteen of them. To see a face you must
look and feel as much as you can. If you skip over, you
must be satisfied with what you have and happily regret
what you miss. I am never happy about missing others'
thoughts. I get bored sometimes and ask: "What's the
point of all this?" I never see the point when I do that;
but I feel it stabbing me.

What about the thoughts of youth? First of all, that
has nothing to do with anything. Life, among other things,
is a circle. Age means everything/nothing/something/all
of these/none of these. You and I are of the same circle;
neither is in front of or behind the other. We are all going
in the same direction, so let's talk about everything and
not feel ashamed. Shame is purple in color. I said that because purple seemed to come to mind. My brother is color
blind. He cannot see reds and greens the way someone in
a book said he should see them. He took a drug one night,
not so long ago, and he saw colors. NOTHING IS WRIT-
TEN.

.   .   .

Empire Bus Lines runs a bus from Poughkeepsie, New York, to New Haven, Connecticut, by way of Danbury, Connecticut, three times a day for four dollars in American currency. If the driver sticks to the route, which does not always happen, you pass a federal prison. The fields in the spring and summer are green and supple. Hills roll up and down for miles with evergreens brocading the summits. Two hundred yards off the paved highway is a fortress, white bricks that block the lines of nature. It is the prison. The bus does not usually stop there. I tense up inside as we pass this leviathan. I cringe with fear. Am I . . . Why here . . . Will I . . . Are they really . . .? Guilty, Innocent, Guilty, Innocent. Questions whose answers are already known. I know that the prison should not exist—man should be free. Prison is a state of mind. So why does the state build a monument to my mind? There is the smell of death and war around that prison. All the life of nature could not blot out that sight. Man can.

I have taken the most available drug substances that seem to be circulating through the arteries of my generation. Artificial stimulants do not expand my mind. I pretend that they do and so it must be so. Why do I pretend? Because lithographing makes egoism vulnerable to chaos, if you know what I mean. The matter of clothing, jargon, style in music, and drug or alcoholic intake are all signs of the times—my, my, how turgid and pretentious I've become. About as much as I care to be; and I know it is the same with you. Did you know that rumor has it that LSD can cause a mutation in human chromosomes which in all probability might make your next child into a pullulating monster? I know why voices are telling me not to be free. Think what might happen! There might be *peace*. Please smile at my youthful chatter. You are very beautiful when you smile and less likely to kill . . . in all probability, which is all or nothing at all that we have to go on. We are rich, you and I. I do not want to see you pretend that you are as poor as I. Blood of my blood, do not fear the monster. Love him and all your days will your house live in everlasting peace. Kill only when you must; but "must" has little meaning. It is a rather elusive word much like the word "elusive." Therefore, to cast the death glance at those bodies to which you gave birth because of an impure blood strain is like choking me in your hands. There is no peace in a house where brother kills brother. *Wonder* at the experience of it all, my brother.

About ten years ago a couple in Maine, USA, joined the march to the sea. Neighbor awoke neighbor at all hours, helped them dress, led themselves out of doors and joined in. The Mainians marched into New Hampshire, Vermont, etcetera, and soon the East Coasters had just about gathered their flock. Virginia took a little more time, but by the first month she had joined the main body and headed West. Illinoians aided Nebraskans and vice versa, until everyone in America was linked up arm in arm singing to the sea. What a magnificent sight when all Americans reached the shores of the Pacific! Some spilled into Baja California, Central and South America, up into Canada and even onto the southern coast of Alaska. Then, everyone's voice chanted out together. You know the rest. Europe marched into Central Europe, in turn, picking up on the Africans, Middle Easterners, until Asia was whirled up and the entire group formed a line on the western shores of the Pacific. Their voices chanted in unison. No one on either side knew what the words meant, but the music, and the faces. Well, you just had to be there. Oh? Well, we can just walk out of doors and see what happens. Do you think your neighbor might JOIN us?

You are my teacher. I am yours. We are all teachers. I cannot tell you anything that you don't already know. All I can give to you is my thanks for your concern, for your smile, for your love. Anything else and I would be faking with you. My and your God, I want to be real. I want you to be real. Ask everything of me. I will do what I can. There is a song sung at the Jewish Passover table. At the end of each verse of the song, your voice rings out *dayanu*. It means, roughly: It will be enough. If I should happen to meet you on the road one day, and perchance I ask you for something, whatever you give—*dayanu*.

You might be angry. You might swear under your breath: "Why doesn't this idealism stop spilling out of the mouth? Change this damn world if you're so goddamn smart. Get off your ass and work for what you want. Only do something and shut your mouth!"

I am doing something. I am working and playing every moment I live, at present. My ideals are none. My vision is clearly blurred. My back is weak . . . but I try. Only I do not know the right way, the best way. I don't even care to know the way. I know what I don't want; now what do I want? See you, feel you, touch you, give to you, take from you. If you strike me, I may get angry. I may even strike back; but that surely is not the way. So let us not provoke each other with lies and blows.

Perhaps/Perhaps not

You are always Welcome
in my house.

HOW
I WON
MY MAJOR WHY*

by
William
Boly

* A "Major Y" is
awarded for competition
at the Varsity level
in a recognized
sport at Yale.
A "Major why,"
on the other hand,
is a pun.

Dear Charlie Reich:

The basic question I want to resolve is whether the cultural revolution and political activism are compatible. The idea of Consciousness III seems to assume that they go hand in hand, but events over the last two years have made me wonder. Paraphrasing, I am skeptical of the capacity of a political activist to lead a healthy, fully human life in this country. I don't mean to distance myself from the problem through aloof diction or erstwhile wit, either. I know I feel the schizophrenia of these two poles within myself and I think I see the same ambivalence at Yale as well.

Whatever follows—observations culled from life last spring at Yale and the past few weeks about campus—is a personal rendition of public events. I do not hesitate to make subjective judgments, conferring on myself the same mantle that you assumed with your original disclaimer last fall. Importantly, these are my impressions alone and are subject to all the vagaries and prejudices of my personality. In short, many who shared these experiences might well disagree with my inferences.

If ever there was an event that belied the prospects of salvation through Consciousness III, the imbroglio at Yale in the spring of 1970 was it. Activity at that time focused on the trial of Bobby Seale. The trial itself became a symbol for the systematic persecution of the Panthers by official branches of the government. On the first weekend in May, thousands of demonstrators came to New Haven to express their support of Chairman Bobby. Yale students had already been on strike for over a week, and the University was "opened up" to accommodate the influx of people.

I sympathized with the "Free Bobby" campaign, because I agreed that our society is racist, that the Panthers have been unfairly hamstrung by arduous legal proceedings on the flimsiest of pretexts, and that, even then, a fair trial may be impossible for a militant Black. Still, hysterical action, which I expected from the right, and witnessed, and which I did not expect from the left, yet witnessed, made categorical support for the strike impossible. The demonstration itself was also disenchanting. The demonstrators who came to New Haven, ostensibly on Seale's behalf, were too erratic even for the Panthers, who sought a decent atmosphere. The demonstrators seemed more concerned with seeking excitement than with helping Bobby. Doug Miranda, local captain of the BPP, spent his evenings with a bull horn urging people to stay off the streets. Sporadic rock- and bottle-throwing persisted.

The demonstrators were by and large veterans of political action. Many came equipped with riot helmets and bandages, for this "demo" was billed on the underground wire as probably a violent one. Some had come to trash the town and university, à la Harvard Square. The open door policy prevented or quelled much resentment, although slogans abounded on walls and sidewalks. One read: "Wake up, Yalies. This place is too damn idyllic." Several small fires were extinguished in the basements of buildings at Yale both the week before and the weekend of the demonstration. There was an explosion at Ingalls Rink, although it is unclear whether it was set by right- or left-wing factions.

The point I'm making is basically emotional. This group of young people greatly disturbed my image of my own generation as essentially humanitarian. After the big demonstration, groups gathered in various colleges to discuss the day's events and plan for the future. Tom Hayden spoke in Jonathan Edwards College. Young, intelligent, articulate and radical, he could not get a hearing from his audience, because he refused to cheerlead an attack on the courthouse. The situation was electric. The greensward was filled to overflowing with people sitting on the hard-packed dirt and a hastily arranged sound system barely carried his voice to the crowd's perimeter. Angry silhouettes rose to challenge his argument that, unlike the Berkeley situation, students could still work with the private university to oppose official violence and suppression.

The argument took an interesting twist. A fellow asked about the bands on the Old Campus that night, and what possible function they had in the tense political atmosphere. The direct clash between developing a youth culture and effective political action was debated. Just before the meeting broke up, Hayden pointed out that the same electricity that powered those guitars and distracted a few hundred demonstrators would fry Bobby if he was found guilty. For once, the audience approved.

The May Day "demo" had a profound effect on Yale's political activity, and it relates also to your optimism about approaching change. Granted, it would never have occurred without the work and idealism of many people. But what about the violent, guilt-ridden young people who came here for excitement, for something that could, as Nathaniel West put it, "make taut their slack minds and bodies"? Certainly, this was not the Consciousness III group of people who know joy, beauty and the simple pleasure of human relations. After observing last May's demonstrators, I will never be so innocent as to expect any one age group to be qualitatively more virtuous than another.

Yale's reaction paralleled my own, perhaps with better reason. Many students had a long summer of normalcy to contrast with the feverish activity of the spring. An obvious gap between an extreme position at Yale and the same position in the summer months led students to a discouraging realization: that it is possible to talk a radical line at school, yet do nothing in the real world. This lack of accountability and a personal sense of hypocrisy have made students more temperate this year. The audience's poise at the Indochina teach-in this winter comes to mind. The audience listened to speakers who were involved in the original commitment to Vietnam and who would have been perfunctorily hissed off the podium in days past. Even when Robert McCloskey dragged out the specter of Russian military prowess as a reason for withdrawing from Vietnam, restraint held sway.

No one wants to venture beyond a position he can live with year round. And that's basically honest. But at the same time that caution, if it stymies all political action, merely places the student prematurely in the position of a family man, unwilling to commit himself because of a responsibility to his "future" or "options."

Anyway, Yale went into shock at what it saw. As the first trial went by, it became clear that the Panthers had misrepresented the extent of their involvement in the Rackley murder. Their avowal of total innocence, made throughout the spring, was badly prejudiced by the conviction of Lonnie McLucas on a lesser charge. Lawyer Garry's figure of twenty-eight Panthers murdered by police was a gross exaggeration calculated to excite support. As a result of many factors, internal and external to the campus, Yale underwent a direct, visceral reaction to last spring. The lack of political activity during the fall reflected a desire for tranquility after the upheaval last year. People talk about how they hope it will be quiet this year.

Still, a problem remains—Yale learned its lesson only too well. And there are issues about which we cannot remain silent, like the WAR. For God's sake, we are now in the most brutal and racist stage of our Indochina involvement. We kill people from the air—tidily, technologically. We phase out ground troops to reduce American casualties, calling it a withdrawal, yet increase bombing, and thereby do little else than change the color of the corpses. What could be more racist than a policy which is calculated on the assumption that Americans will accept Asians dying indefinitely, but will not allow continued American deaths?

You know all this. But sometimes it slips to the back of the mind, and needs to be recalled. The antiwar movement has done some good. As Al Lowenstein points out, it's not a matter of whether, but now a question of when we leave Vietnam. Meanwhile, the lack of pressure from the people is allowing a last, thrashing, death-spasm of destruction by air-power in Laos, Cambodia and Vietnam.

So, here's the cruncher—Kingman Brewster didn't know the half of it when he labeled the quiet on campus an "eerie silence." The only way that lack of political activity could be construed as healthy was through your analysis of a cultural revolution which was transforming the basis of society, and which would eliminate the very sources of war, ecocide, and racism. But students cannot afford to use the idea of a revolution in consciousness as an adequate response to the active immorality of Vietnam. A recent cartoon in *The Phoenix* shows a student lying in bed, with eyes closed and earphones on, a peace sign fallen from his hands. Over him in a paternalistic stance, shushing with one hand any would-be Prince Charmings, is our President, who clutches in his other hand a bomber that rains neatly patterned canister-death over Indochina. The caption reads: "Student opinion about the war has undergone a radical transformation." The conclusion is clear: Students cannot ignore Vietnam, because there is no distinguishing between the development of a new life-style and callous apathy. Consequently, the war infects youth culture, and will destroy us if we continue to content ourselves with rejecting it privately while not taking positive action against it.

I canvassed the students of Jonathan Edwards a couple of weeks ago on behalf of the People's Peace Treaty. Nearly everyone agreed to sign the treaty, because nearly everyone feels strongly about the war. But, when it came to implementing the treaty with positive action, a general reluctance emerged. The treaty as a petition has no significance. In order for a signature to mean something on the treaty, the individual must make a symbolic commitment to separate himself from the war. And that's where I lost most students' eyes.

The treaty purports to make peace between the individual and the Vietnamese. In my estimation, signing it commits one to no longer support the nation's warmaking efforts, even tacitly, and obligates one to work against the war. Therefore, a senior who endorses the treaty forswears joining the reserves, and either files for a C.O. or resists induction. Everyone else should refuse to pay taxes, canvass in the community, participate in antiwar rallies, and pressure Congress with letters, while gearing towards the '72 elections.

That's a pretty difficult line to market at Yale this year. Particularly because of last spring. I knew the people I canvassed and obviously got straight answers. One individual stands out in my mind. He is a tall, sensitive sophomore who reminisced about May Day and spoke of how disillusioning the whole strike experience had been. His main tenet was that the individual is powerless to change our society. His thinking differed so profoundly from the average person's (middle American) that he would not know where to begin in opening a discussion about the war. In other words, like you, he perceived the problem as organic, but this perception has led to a despair of acting to change things. It is ironic that I was unsuccessful in awakening this fellow to the personal responsibility we each have regarding the war. For, by any standards of life-style, he is more radical than I. This guy claims he will either refuse induction or go to Canada, but in any event, he intends to face the problem individually. I think his attitudes speak eloquently of the impotent, bitter and finally resigned attitude on campus.

Another sophomore insisted on signing the treaty, even though he considered it just another petition. "It's just a piece of paper unless you do something about it," I said. "It's just a piece of paper then." He had marched on Washington before, and no longer believed such strategies worth his time. The peace movement needs new, inventive actions to reenlist people who are sympathetic.

Beyond that, can we afford the luxury of waiting for the revolution in consciousness? Right now, sitting back is killing the good feeling that existed in our guts just a little while ago. Vietnam can be ignored. It can be put in the back of our minds where it settles uneasily, corroding and festering at our pride and idealism. Vietnam testifies to our impotence as long as we do nothing, and most of all, it makes of all our rich culture—the music, craft, dance—a distracting plaything. That's right. The culture is no more than a rattle to appease the teething baby. Youth has cut its gums on Vietnam for too long, and it's time we bared our hard-won teeth and obtained justice.

Enough rant. Consider Yale's students for a moment. The teach-in was proclaimed a success because of the number of students who attended it. Nonsense. A teach-in constitutes the absolute minimum level of political participation. Attendance at a teach-in tells the world that you have a curiosity, an interest, even a concern over the topic under discussion. Yet Woolsey Hall was not full that evening, and I've seen it bursting for a number of rock groups. Furthermore, at least one-quarter of the crowd consisted of older people. Therefore, the better part of Yale's undergraduates didn't even express a minimum level of concern over the war.

I was impressed by the speakers, and exhilarated to witness the reawakening of an organized antiwar movement. Those who attended shared that sense of rededication. But the majority that hadn't bothered to come, many my friends, sobered me back to one brand of gimlet-eyed reality. An active resentment, a scepticism greeted us in the dorm. "Naïve," "God help me but you're easy prey for a demagogue," and "I've seen it all before." The next day at lunch I was waiting in line for my daily bread with a good friend. "Did you break wind last night?" he asked.

I did not catch his meaning, and asked him to repeat himself.

"Did you break wind last night?" and this time his smile made me think of the teach-in's slogan, "We're going to break the silence." A joke.

I couldn't laugh, and I still can't laugh.

That introduces the most terrible aspect of political activism—the loss of a sense of humor. I watched last May as my friends became more and more hypnotically absorbed in the Panther question. I remember the feeling of estrangement as they went further along a political road that I was either unable or unwilling to tread. Friends became strangers, because they believed a truth I did not, and since I would not boycott classes for no clearly stated purpose, they felt an impatience at what must have seemed sheer obstinacy.

Now the shoe is on the other foot. The war rankles everyone, but some can sublimate better than others its toll of moral bankruptcy. The degree of politicization (here's some fuel for the cynics) is almost a direct function of vulnerability to the draft. This matter gives the lie to a portrayal of idealized youth pursuing the path of righteousness in the face of amoral ogre-leaders. Students have proved themselves as pragmatically oriented and as ripe a material for cooptation as any age group. In Jonathan Edwards, seniors facing the draft show by far the most concern about Vietnam. Seniors largely make up the Wednesday evening study group. Among seniors those with numbers below 195 show strong concern about developments in the war zone and administration policy. Some individuals, oddly enough with numbers above the magic 195, resent the introduction of the war into their bright college years. I am no exception. My low draft number has "radicalized" me, just as a higher one would have neutralized me. Oh well, young people are only human, but I repeat, they are human, and the idealized image you sometimes project denies that obvious fact.

My problem, then, is how to maintain a sense of humor along with an immediate feeling about the war; how to remain human and aware. A balance in these two areas is important because I see the cultural revolution as the necessary validation of political activism.

The problem does finally reduce itself to human terms. Two of my closest friends—roommates for three years in college—have high draft numbers. One is totally apolitical and kids me about my button-pushing, study-grouping ways in the last few weeks. But beneath the joking, a real separation has developed between us, because he refuses to consider seriously his role in a problem that involves us all. I have learned not to discuss the war when he's around, because he is determined to remain uninvolved, and the subject only aggravates our differences. The question, then, becomes whether a friendship with those kinds of restrictions is worth having.

I would say that the radical segment of Jonathan Edwards is the most isolated and inbred in the college. It's much easier for me to see how that evolved in light of my recent experience. Perhaps the tendency is inevitably towards a psychic isolation, but since it also brings an attendant loss of perspective and sense of humor and humanity, it must be avoided. My other good friend with a high number has kept pace with me in studying the Indochina problem, despite the fact that he comes from a fairly conservative home. He has an open mind and a concern for the moral implications of his decisions. He even wishes that he had a low draft number so that the situation confronted him and made him absolutely define his beliefs with his actions.

So, the trade-off is between a personal sense of integrity and a certain openness and social balance. Bella Abzug impressed me very much at the teach-in as someone who could bring a smile and be serious, so that her abundant human warmth was shown to be the soul of her political convictions.

Life can be led, in other words, and I would posit that

it can be led with greater sanity outside the university. Perhaps I'm deluding myself, but when my decision about the war really determines my future, I can then be convinced that my separation from (intolerance for?) less involved people reflects a commitment. In other words, I can approach people with a firm sense of my own honesty, of my consistency between word and deed. In school, it's too easy to speak a radical line and preserve your options for the future. Next year, that kind of hypocrisy won't be possible.

FAMILY JOURNEYS:

SIGHTS
SEEN

by
Michael
Gecan

Originally published in
The New Journal, Vol.
Two, number ten,
April 27, 1969.

*To take a meaning from experience
and try to make it active is, in
fact, our process of growth. Some
of these meanings we receive and
re-create. Others we must make
for ourselves and try to communicate.
The human crisis is always a crisis of
understanding.*

*Raymond Williams**

* *Culture and Society* (New York: Harper and Row, Publishers, 1966).

PART I

Ah, Mike," my father said to me, "you always seem to be leaving us."

We sat in the Café Moravia, a Bohemian restaurant just west of Chicago, and ate a fine Sunday dinner. Three days before, on Christmas Eve, I had asked that we all go out for a meal before I returned to the East. Everyone had agreed. So now my mother and sister Barbara were there, as were my uncle and aunt and cousin Cathy. The conversation was quiet and low-keyed: they saying that they wished I would stay for one more week, that I was always running off *somewhere;* and I telling them that I *had* enjoyed my two weeks at home, but hoped to visit friends in Washington and Tennessee and spend some days in the Smoky Mountains, in a cabin there, alone.

The table was cleared. My father raised his glass and proposed a toast: "To our family." We nodded, smiled our agreement to the proposition, and sipped the white wine.

Three hours later, while being conveyed by car across western Indiana through a bleak gray industrial dusk, I thought about my father. He had walked me to my friend's car and, after my bag had been shoved into the trunk, had taken my hand and wished me well. Was there anything I needed? he had asked. No, everything was fine. Was I sure? Yeah.

PART II

In 1928 my father was fifteen years old and enrolled in a
military school in Zagreb. Three years before he had won
a scholarship to the school and had left his home village,
located on the Adriatic near Ruyeke, and journeyed to the
big city. In the winter of his final year at the school he was
looking forward to graduation. He would soon be the first
member of his family to earn a high school diploma.

Those years in Zagreb were exciting. He did quite
well in his classwork, made many friends, and was a champion soccer player, something of a star. He knew both
poverty and relative ease; he understood both life on the
farm and life in the city; he was confident of his own
abilities and aware of his enormous stores of energy.

One day he was directed by his school superior to go
to the visitors' room. He was surprised; apparently someone had come to see him. When he opened the door to the
guestroom he saw his mother. She was dressed in her best
clothes; a small traveling bag was at her feet. He worried that something must be wrong. Was sister sick? His
mother said that nothing was wrong, really; but she refused to come directly to the point. After they had chatted
for a while, she said it: she had received a letter from her
husband, who was then living in America. He had left
Croatia several months before his son's birth; August had
never seen his father's face. In the letter her husband
commanded that August be sent to America immediately.
She had come to Zagreb to fetch him. They were to return
to the village and prepare him for his departure.

There was more than surprise in August's eyes when
he heard his mother deliver her message. Exhilaration and
fear, anticipation and disappointment rushed up through

him. Such an adventure: to travel, alone, to America. And such a loss: to leave one's friends and family and successes behind and begin again. He would pass across thousands of miles, to a monstrous city, to a father whom he had never known.

Several weeks later he stood in Union Station in Chicago and looked around. He thought perhaps someone would meet him, perhaps his father would be there. No one appeared. August walked and, after a time, after asking several people for directions, taking wrong turns, and avoiding a clash with some toughs, he came upon his father's house. He mounted the front steps and knocked on the door. It opened. Father and son saw one another for the first time. They found that they had little to say. August's visions of ice cream, candy, and cake were quickly undercut by bland reality—a bowl of barley soup. His father told him to eat and then to get some sleep. All, August included, would be going to work very early the next morning.

PART III

In the spring of 1913 August's father, my grandfather, was living in Croatia and hearing some tantalizing tales. Friends and relatives from the local villages had emigrated to America, to Chicago and Pittsburgh particularly, and had begun to build new lives there. They wrote letters to my grandfather—letters which described the conditions in America and which, while sure to mention the crowding and dirt and horrors of city and factory life, also alluded to the amounts of money made and the comforts enjoyed and the security of good steady work. My grandfather was intrigued, but for many months resisted the temptation.

My grandfather was a tough man—muscular, hard-working, and often cruel. The battle he waged against his land and vineyards seemed to result in a draw at best. He and his family survived; but he could not get ahead, could never pin the elements down and win for himself some profit and rest. The temptation soon proved to be too great. He had money enough to finance one person's passage to America. He decided to go alone, promising to work very hard and to save as much money as he possibly could. He said that he would send for his wife and children at the earliest opportunity.

When he arrived in America he sought out those Croatians who had clustered on the Near-West Side of Chicago. There he lived, in an old frame house infested by roaches and rats, with four other immigrant men. One of the four persuaded an official of the Chicago and Northwestern Railroad to hire my grandfather. Without proximate family, with few friends, and with a desperate desire to succeed, my grandfather devoted most of his time to his job.

Years passed. My grandfather worked seventy hours each week and won a reputation. His ferocity and determination attracted the attention of the railroad bosses. His pay was increased. He was promoted once, then again. In 1920 he was named a gang foreman. He saved and saved, lived in pathetic squalor, never dared to ask for a vacation, and then, ten years after he had left Yugoslavia, wrote to his wife and requested that she and the children join him.

His wife and daughter arrived in 1924. The son, then ten years old, was left behind to be cared for by relatives. The city shocked my grandmother; the crowds and noise and filth disgusted her. She became quite ill, blamed the city for her illness, and decided to return to Croatia. She asked her husband if he would like to accompany them. He had made a sizable sum of money; they would certainly live more comfortably now. My grandfather considered the proposition but then said, no, he had not made enough. He would remain in America, alone, if need be. But he knew of one possible companion: his son. In 1928 he judged that August was finally old enough and probably strong enough to be put to work.

On the day following August's arrival in Chicago, father led son to the local railroad yard and described the task which August would be performing. August was to serve as a water boy for the gangs of men who worked repairing the rails. A worker one day complained that the water boy was loafing. My grandfather called August to him, screamed at him as they stood before a crowd of workers, hit him across the face, and then fired him. The worker had been mistaken, but my grandfather refused to listen to his son's self-defense.

August found another job and continued to live with his father and the other men. They rarely saw the sights of the city, rarely ventured from their neighborhood. Their home was always in need of some major repair. They ate the foods of the old country—barley and bread.

Early in 1935 August's father took a trip to Yugoslavia. He had safely weathered the depression. In fact, his salary had doubled during those past four years; he took home more than sixty dollars each week, which was fine pay in those days. During his stay in the Old Country, the Yugoslav bank into which he had deposited all of his money was closed; the money was claimed by the government. My grandfather lost more than twenty-three thousand dollars. Two miserable months later he died of a heart attack.

PART IV

Some weeks ago I was alone in Tennessee; for seven days lived high up in the Smokies; there wrote and read and walked among the hills; there thought, wondered: What exactly *was* it in those men—whose pasts and lives held something out to me, some elements of meaning—what was so common to their histories? Not, I hope, in any rage for order, but in a straight attempt to understand, I saw a pattern, an aid to understanding.

I saw first this image:

My grandfather says goodbye to his wife and child; he brings the traveling bag to his shoulder, waves, and then slowly walks from his Croatian home and out along the road to Trieste. The village is behind him now, America ahead. He leaves, to his relief, the cramped quarters of village and farm life. At the same time he is sad to surrender so much of the community of friends and relatives he has known since his childhood. He denies himself the joys and sorrows of raising his own children. He deprives himself of his wife's company. He chooses to live and to work in another country.

This image is the first part of a pattern. The second part covers a longer period of time—my grandfather's first years in America. He knew, when he left Croatia, that the work would be hard and the life lonely. But, during those first years, he harbored a hope: that he and his wife and children would be bettered by his efforts. He had immigrated for *their* benefit; he was working and scrimping for *them;* and he was looking forward to the day of their reunion. His hopes were battered during these years, but they endured.

The second part pushes imperceptibly into the third. In this stretch of time, my grandfather began to lose sight of his initial hopes and ambitions. His family faded from view. By 1923 he had not seen his wife for ten years. He had never seen his son; and his daughter was, by this time, a different girl. Work and money became his major preoccupations.

The pattern is completed by a fourth and final part: my grandfather's financial disaster and subsequent death.

As I set these thoughts down for the first time, I realized that the pattern had been retraced, with some minor modifications, by my father. Then, on one cold Tennessee night, I saw with a shock that this same pattern was and is influencing me.

PART V

My grandfather's hopes had a momentum which maintained itself for many years. His desire to improve the lives of his wife and children was tied to a more general ambition: that he would, in the process of elevating his own family, be proving the worth of all Croatians and of the Croatian heritage as a whole. In Chicago, he lived, worked, and played among fellow Croatians; in this way he was constantly reminded of his declared devotion to his family. These everyday reminders helped to keep those hopes alive.

My father harbored similar hopes when he arrived in America. He wished to see his mother and sister again and wanted to return to his relatives and friends in the village. He worked hard, quite hard, but also continued to cultivate his rich heritage.

After his father's death August moved to another section of the West Side, into a pocket of people who had emigrated from the same section of Croatia. Croatian was the primary language spoken in this section. A Croatian social club was the center of neighborhood activity. The younger men formed soccer and softball teams. Most of the men worked together in small groups in the railroad yards or in construction gangs. And all attended the same Croatian-language Church. Within this closed community August lived. In 1936 he married a Croatian girl. He began to work for a construction company. He continued to play soccer. He traveled throughout the city as the bass player in a Croatian band.

Then he went to war. He tried to suppress his thick Slavic accent and to sharpen his English. To be mistaken for a German was not uncommon, and could well be disastrous. Late in 1944, my father was captured and imprisoned by the troops of General Patton's Fifth Armored Division. They had found him lying in a German hospital in serious condition. His accent led them to believe that he was an enemy, and a Mississippi sergeant broke my father's nose with the butt of a rifle. Several days later the Americans discovered that my father was on their side.

While my father lay in a hospital with shrapnel lodged in his back and a nose just recently broken, my mother was involved in a skirmish of her own. She was stepping from the tight security of the Croatian community and out into the larger surrounding world. She hopped on a bus each morning and rode to a factory. There she met second-, third-, and fourth-generation Americans. Her ethnicity suddenly seemed to be of less importance. She, like my father, was asked to conform, to be more American and middle class.

My grandfather took one giant step, across an ocean, away from his Croatian heritage and family. In subsequent years he stepped farther and farther from that past, until it lost the shape and substance of reality and resembled, more and more, a dream, or an unexpected letter from a distant and not very intimate friend. My father also took that giant step. But *his* and my mother's departure from their shared past was more gradual. The conforming pressures felt during wartime increased the pace of their departure. After the war their *work* continued the process.

In 1945 my father was flown back to the States. He returned with several tender scars, a purple heart, a silver star, and stinging memories of the Battle of the Bulge. He lay for eleven months in the convalescent wards of several hospitals. Then, when sufficiently healed, he packed away his uniform, medals, and memorabilia, and walked to work. And he didn't dawdle along the way. There was little opportunity for that. I was born in 1949, my sister in 1952. My grandmother depended upon my parents for support. The family always needed money: for the babies, for the children's educations, for hospital bills. My mother and father accepted their responsibility; they worked with dogged determination.

After many years in the construction trade, my father decided to buy a tavern. In 1953 we became the proud owners of a bar located at an excellent intersection just two blocks from our home. My father tended bar; my mother cooked hot lunches for the railroad workers and anyone else who might stop in; and I, when I was old enough (five, that is), served the food and drinks to our customers. It was a fine time. Our friends and neighbors, Croatians and non-Croatians alike, would gather at our place to eat and drink and sometimes sing. Many pleasant evenings were passed there. Then my mother became seriously sick and entered a hospital. The bills mounted. One Sunday the local Mafia representative stepped into our place and asked my father for the regular monthly payment (we paid them for "protection"; we also paid the police department for "protection"; the fire department, too). My father said that we didn't have the money. The collector demanded that the tavern be closed, or else. Knowing full well what "or else" might mean (a firebomb through our Pabst Blue Ribbon windows), we locked up for the last time that night and never returned. My father went back to his construction work, but the labor proved too harsh. For the last twelve years he has worked as a nightwatchman and security guard in several banks and electronics companies.

PART VI

My father's mother died in 1962. The letter—addressed to my father, written in the flowing style of his older sister— arrived on a warm Spring day. My father came home late in the afternoon, picked up the unopened envelope, and went into the living room. After some time I peeked through the half-closed door and saw him sitting in the dull light next to the window with his head in his hands. He did not cry, just sat and stared. He called me to him and picked a photograph from his wallet. His mother was sitting, wearing a gray ankle-length dress. Her long black hair was pulled tightly back; her dark eyes were without expression.

Standing beside her chair was my father, dressed in the uniform of his academy. My father said that thirty years had passed since he had last seen his mother. Long ago he had promised to return to her. She had asked that he return. He told me that he had betrayed her in some way. Then he began to cry.

The boy in the photograph and the man who left Chicago for Fort Sheridan in 1942 were much the same. They both loved music, loved to sing, to dance, to play the bass. Both were healthy and athletic and appreciated natural beauty. Both respected their family, community, and ethnicity.

But the man who returned from the war and who sat in the chair mourning the death of his mother had known significant change. His war wounds had claimed a lung, and a construction accident had cost him his large toe and left him with a permanent limp. He had been exhausted by an endless series of twelve-hour days and sixty-five-hour work weeks. He was too tired to play his bass often, too weary to read a book or walk along the beach or explore the local forest area. He had been beaten, psychologically, by his efforts to keep his family above a minimal financial waterline—by abusive bosses, by sponging mafiosi, by a neighborhood which was changing racially and from which he could not move, and by the great distances which sometimes seemed to separate him from me and my sister. We found that we had little to say to one another. None of us could understand the nature of the distance.

PART VII

The simple fact is this: my father and I were simply not very close during my grade school and high school years. He worked much of the time. And when he returned to the house, late in the evening, or on Sundays, he wished—not to kick a soccer ball around a field, or to teach me the rudiments of the bass, or to give an informal lesson in Croatian language or history—but rather to relax, to sit down and drink a beer and talk with his friends.

But the fact of my father's devotion to his job and of his natural exhaustion was not, alone, responsible for the distance that grew between us. Two other elements were involved. First, my father did not consider it essential that our Croatian heritage be taught to me. He tried at times to transmit some aspects of the heritage. But if I resisted these attempts (and I did: why learn how to play a big old bass when I could be out playing basketball?), I was always allowed to go my own way. Because his accent and Yugoslav education had done him so little good, he never insisted that I learn to speak the language. He had been denied jobs; he had been abused during the war; and recently he had been denied a promotion (from watchman to warehouse manager, with a doubling of salary), because he could not write the English language well enough to suit his boss. His heritage had brought him grief and frustration, and he was wary of it. He could not see how such a heritage could help me; it might even do some harm. My parents did not want my sister and me to suffer as they had suffered. We were to be good, well-educated, well-integrated Americans.

The second element is closely related to the first. My father knew that *he* was not equipped to teach Barbara and me to be truly American. But he *did* believe that society, for a price, would provide us with all that we might need. He sent us to a Catholic grade school and Catholic high schools. I joined the Cub Scouts so that I might learn to enjoy nature—learn to walk in the woods, tie ropes, recognize flowers. The local Little League provided a beautiful uniform, catcher's equipment, and teammates. The Off-the-Street Club tried to keep me off the goddamn streets. I went to a nun for piano lessons, to the Park District for swimming lessons, to high school for instruction in the Russian language. And for the money with which all these benefits were bought I went to father.

PART VIII

My grandfather heard, and responded to, this call:

> Leave your country and family, Don't worry; your children and wife will be cared for by the villagers. Go to America and there work, work hard. For, in that way, the lives of both you and your loved ones will be bettered.

My grandfather simply failed to foresee the consequences of his immediate and gradual departures. He never imagined that he would someday surrender completely to the attractions of his job and his salary. Nor did he imagine that the emotional distance between himself and his family would grow so great. Due to circumstance and his own weakness, the distance *did* increase. And his departure—initially an act of self-sacrifice and devotion—resembled more, as time passed, an act of desertion.

My father listened to a similar, slightly modified message:

Leave your mother and school and friends and go to America. There work. And when you have a family of your own do not give your rich heritage to your children. No. Rather, leave them in the hands of society, which will educate and socialize them while you are away. Go off to your factory or warehouse or office. Work hard, as hard as you possibly can. For in that way, you and your wife and children will be bettered.

My father, who loved us dearly, thought that he could best prove his love by working and earning money. He was, first and foremost, a breadwinner. I was the child of those institutions which, all too often, stood in his stead.

Society has always said to me:

Leave your family and neighborhood and friends and go to Yale. There work, study hard, and eventually move on to graduate school or law school or a well-paying job. Your parents are quite capable of caring for themselves. You must simply proceed alone, or with a wife, up the ladder toward your special brand of success. In *that* way you and your parents will find fulfillment and happiness.

My grandfather's response was most dramatic. He stepped *bodily* from his family and lived in lonely exile, working and hoarding. But my father also emigrated from the family circle. His was a spiritual migration. Each day he took himself from the context of our home and established a temporary residence in another land—the land of labor. In his warehouse, standing before a door checking security passes, he was condemned to an exile as lonely as his father's.

I too have begun to separate my self from my family and my past. During my years at Yale I have lost sight of my initial hopes to better both myself and my parents. I have become more and more preoccupied with a single end: self-advancement up a ladder of academic and social merit. Like my grandfather and father, I am on a ladder, alone, climbing toward the top.

This pattern of an isolated individual clinging to a ladder and forgetting those who stand at the ladder's base, leans on several pivotal presumptions. It is presumed that, after graduation, I will walk alone into the world and find an appropriate ladder. Though I will be expected to love my family and neighborhood and to visit my Chicago home occasionally, it is also presumed that I will never really return to them.

These presumptions are pernicious. *Not* because they encourage an individual immigrant or factory worker or student to stand alone. Perhaps each of us needs to meet the world face to face, without the help of our family and friends; and it is possible, perhaps likely, that many of us will stand alone for much of our lives. And *not* because the presumptions encourage us to send gifts—paychecks, diplomas, awards—as emblems of our affection. Such gifts, if kept in the proper perspective, are fine forms of expressed friendship. These presumptions are pernicious because the pattern, having become too dominant, has dwarfed other, equally valid ways of life; and because devotion to the pattern deadens the believing individual and disrupts families.

PART IX

The image of the isolated individual is, says Raymond Williams, "objectionable in two related respects: first, that it weakens the principle of common betterment which ought to be an absolute value; second, that it sweetens the poison of hierarchy, in particular by offering the hierarchy of merit as a thing different in kind from the hierarchy of money and birth."

When my grandfather, father, and I began our separate climbs, we held firmly in mind the notions of family betterment and social equality. During the courses of our climbs the notions tended to fade. Meanwhile our families were weakened by our departures and were in danger of disintegration. And we, the rising individuals, found that we were receiving blessings which were, at best, quite mixed.

My grandfather was a gifted man: strong, ferocious, loyal to those whom he loved. His energies were chewed up by his job and wasted when he discovered that those to whom he most wanted to give were not there to accept his gifts. My father was a gifted man: a fine athlete, an intelligent student, an excellent musician, a warm and loving member of a Croatian clan. He retains many of his gifts, but some have been lost because he has lived too long in the land of labor and has not had the opportunity to exercise his vitalities. He has had to work. And I have certain gifts. I like to study and to write. Some high school teachers, together with friends in Chicago and friends and professors here at Yale, have pushed and prodded me and shown me the values and limitations of academic life.

The danger now is that I will waste what I have— will let my gifts be withered by years of futile loneliness, or by graduate training which is overly rigorous and deadeningly dull, or by selfish hoarding and self-seeking. The danger now is that I will, without considering the alternatives, take another step up a ladder and, in effect, reject those to whom I owe my deepest love and most enduring commitment.

PART X

I do not propose that we all march back to our homes with the banners of knowledge rippling in the breeze and the bugles of culture blaring. No. I propose that we knock at the doors of our homes and neighborhoods and that, when the door is opened and we are face to face with our fathers and mothers and friends, we offer them some part of what we are: our limited and specialized knowledge, our powers of analysis and criticism, our love for art, our youth, our energy, our clumsy love.

ABOUT THE CONTRIBUTORS

David Darlington, a junior at Yale, lives in New Shrewsbury, New Jersey. He reports that recently, while at home for a short visit, he cut the grass without being told to do so.

Daniel Peters is married and living in Vancouver, British Columbia. Last year he attended the graduate school in English in Vancouver. This year he is writing fiction.

John S. Rolander is a Yale senior who hopes to attend medical school in the coming year. He and his family live in Switzerland.

Donald D. Lindley, whose family lives in Milwaukee, was a member of the Yale class of 1971. He plans to attend graduate school in journalism.

Mary Wilke is a senior at Yale. Majoring in psychology, she is also studying literature. She hopes to teach, either in the United States or England.

Scott Stoner, one-time American Studies major, grew up on the banks of the Delaware in New Jersey. He dropped out of Yale in the winter of 1970 to seek, as he put it, "black tulips and blue dahlias growing wild along the American roadside." He has recently resigned himself to the life of a tennis professional and rock'n'roll god.

Bill Littlefield, Jr., is now teaching literature at the Lawrenceville School in Lawrenceville, New Jersey. He is at work writing both fiction and literary criticism.

Robert Walker, of Oklahoma, is now married and serving in the armed forces.

Leigh Crystal is a senior at Yale. Her home is in New Jersey. A psychology major, she is equally interested in literature and philosophy.

Charles A. Pidano, Jr., spent the past year living and working in Boston, Massachusetts. He is now on the West Coast, traveling and searching for something of interest to do.

Robert H. Rettew is about to complete his senior year at Yale.

Thomas E. Seus spent the past year in Germany, as an officer in the United States Army. He hopes to attend law school in the United States.

Jonathan Sternberg, a Yale graduate, has completed his first year in law school and is living in Boston. He may resume his writing in the months ahead.

Ralph Halsey lives in Woodbridge, Connecticut.

Peter Mareneck is working and living in his commune near New Haven, Connecticut. He is a junior at Yale.

Charles H. Levin was graduated from Yale in June, 1971. At present he is living in Los Angeles. An actor, he is looking for work with a theater group.

William Boly is a member of the Peace Corps and is now teaching literature in Afghanistan.

Michael Gecan is living in Chicago, Illinois, and is working on a novel.

Date Due

Due	Returned	Due	Returned
FEB 0 9 1990	FEB - 9 1990		
MAR 2			
MAR 2 1990	MAR 0 5 1990		